San Francisco Giants IQ

The Ultimate Test of True Fandom

Tucker Elliot & Zac Robinson

Copyright © 2018 Tucker Elliot, Zac Robinson.
All rights reserved.
ISBN: 978-0-9883648-6-8
Cover design by Holly Walden Ross.
Front cover photo courtesy of Mark Whitt.
Interior layout and formatting by BMP Digital.
Black Mesa
Florida

CONTENTS

	INTRODUCTION	1
1	THE NUMBERS GAME	5
2	BASEBALL QUOTES	17
3	FRANCHISE RECORDS	29
4	OCTOBER BASEBALL	41
5	THE SLUGGERS	53
6	THE HURLERS	65
7	FANTASTIC FEATS	77
8	AWARD WINNERS	89
9	THE TEAMS	101
10	EXTRA INNINGS	113

INTRODUCTION

THE New York Gothams began play on a field located at 110th street and Sixth Avenue—a field where polo matches had previously been held—on May 1, 1883, and with that game, the Polo Grounds and the franchise soon to be known as the Giants came into existence.

The club used several different ballparks in the early years.

Four were known by the iconic name Polo Grounds. It was at the third Polo Grounds where the franchise claimed its first modern World Series title in 1905, but during the 1954 World Series it was at the fourth Polo Grounds where Willie Mays made "The Catch."

There is a lot of history in the Giants franchise.

The title won by the 1905 club was the first for any National League team in baseball's modern era—and overall, the Giants claimed five world championship titles during the New York-era of franchise history. In a half-century of play after moving to San Francisco in 1958, the Giants made it to the postseason eight times and won three additional pennants … but it was the 2010 club that made history with the first world championship in the San Francisco-era of Giants history.

Ask any fan to name "great" baseball franchises and you will surely hear the Chicago Cubs, Los Angeles Dodgers, Boston Red Sox, and New York Yankees … but here is a fun fact: none of those teams have won as many regular season games as the Giants. In fact, the Giants have the most regular season wins of any team in the history of organized sports—period.

It gets better.

The Giants can "drop" names with the best of them. As spring training got underway in February 2009, Giants MLB.com beat writer Chris Haft perfectly illustrated this very point with a blog titled, "Now we know it's baseball season: Mays is here." He went on to write: "The Giants were graced Monday by the arrival of Willie Howard Mays, who needs no introduction."

No kidding.

In baseball history, more Hall of Fame players suited up for the Giants than for any other franchise—including the New York Yankees and Boston Red Sox—and a quick glimpse at just a partial list of those players is awe-inspiring: Orlando Cepeda, Monte Irvin, Willie Mays, Willie McCovey, Mel

Ott, Bill Terry, Monte Ward, Carl Hubbell, Juan Marichal, Christy Mathewson, and John McGraw.

This is a book of history and trivia.

Its purpose is to celebrate this historic franchise and its iconic players. In these pages you will find Hall of Fame legends, award-winners, postseason triumphs, fan-favorite players, awe-inspiring performances … the glory, passion, and emotion that the greatest moments in franchise history evoke.

Sit back and reminisce.

It's your San Francisco Giants IQ, the ultimate test of true fandom.

Enjoy.

When he [Willie McCovey] belts a home run he does it with such authority it seems like an act of God.
                                                            Walter Alston

1

THE nearly 40,000-strong crowd stood and held their collective breath as High Pocket Kelly settled his lanky frame into the right-handed batters box and eyed the man on the mound, Bullet Joe Bush. The Yankee righty clung to a 3-2 lead, but now with two outs the bases were loaded and he was tired.

High Pocket got his pitch and served it into left-center, scoring two runs and giving the Giants the lead for good. They added another run and claimed the 1922 World Series title four games to none (with a tie in game two).

The fifth game was played at the Polo Grounds on October 8th. It was the last time the Giants won a World Series at home.

—

Charles M. Schulz was born seven weeks later in Minneapolis, Minnesota. Schulz grew up in St. Paul with a brief stint in Needles, California.

He is, of course, known for giving us the lovable loser, Charlie Brown. The Peanuts comic strip launched on October 2, 1950, a day after the New York Giants ended their season with a 5-1 win over Boston.

In 1958, Schulz made the move out west right along with the Giants. He settled in Sebastopol, some 50 miles north of San Francisco (many years later he moved to Santa Rosa). It was in Sebastopol that he became a Giants fan, so much so that he even wrote about Hall of Famer Willie McCovey in one of his comic strips. In it, Charlie Brown lamented to Linus, asking why McCovey couldn't have hit the ball three feet higher.

The comic was in reference to the Game 7 line drive that would have given the Giants the 1962 World Series title if it wasn't snagged by Yankee second baseman, Bobby Richardson.

Schulz never got to see the San Francisco Giants celebrate a world championship. He passed away a decade before the title drought ended in 2010.

However, as did every other Giants fan of his generation ... he saw a lot of history. He witnessed Roger Craig manage the 1989 Giants to a pennant behind the sweet swing of lefty Will Clark ... Kevin Mitchell, and his barehanded grab in left field ... Juan Marichal fire the first San Francisco no-hitter in 1963 ... and just three weeks later the greatest game ever pitched when Marichal and Warren Spahn delivered an unbelievable pitcher's duel ... Willie McCovey and Willie Mays smacking home runs ... Candy Maldonado and his 1987 cycle ...

And so much more.

Much like Charles Schulz and his Peanuts, this baseball franchise is steeped in greatness. No other team has won more games than the Giants. The franchise is a who's who list of spectacular players. And Giants fans are the best in the world.

...

Let's get started with the trivia. In the first inning we play "The Numbers Game" ... do you know the jersey numbers for these all-time greats?

SAN FRANCISCO GIANTS IQ

TOP OF THE FIRST

Q1: The Hall of Fame's inaugural class of 1936 had just five inductees: Ty Cobb, Walter Johnson, Babe Ruth, Honus Wagner, and New York Giants legend Christy Mathewson. Mathewson's career highlights include 12 consecutive 20-win seasons and four 30-win seasons. He's a member of Major League Baseball's All-Century Team and widely considered the greatest pitcher in history. He didn't have a uniform number. Instead the Giants hang a "NY" in his honor. What is the franchise record number of games that Christy Mathewson won for the New York Giants?
   a) 366
   b) 369
   c) 372
   d) 375

Q2: Hall of Fame manager John McGraw earned the nickname "Little Napoleon" because of his stature and demeanor. McGraw stood only 5-foot-7 and weighed 155 pounds, but his fiery, competitive spirit inspired his teams to dominate the NL for the better part of three decades. In 29 full seasons with McGraw as manager, the Giants placed first or second an astounding 21 times—and for that the Giants hang a "NY" in his honor. How many times did McGraw's Giants win the pennant?
   a) 8
   b) 10
   c) 12
   d) 14

Q3: Hall of Fame legend Bill Terry was one of the most extraordinary player/managers in baseball history. As a first baseman he led the Giants in batting average every year from 1929-35, and he never hit worse than .320 during any of the nine seasons in which he had at least 500 at-bats. As a player/manager, Terry won the 1933 World Series. What is the number retired by the Giants in honor of Bill Terry?
   a) 3
   b) 13
   c) 23

d) 33

Q4: Mel Ott was an 11-time All-Star during 22 seasons with the Giants. He was just a 17-year-old kid when he debuted in 1926, but when he hung up his spikes for good in 1947 he was the franchise leader in games, at-bats, runs, RBIs, hits, doubles, and home runs. What is the number retired by the Giants in honor of Mel Ott?
- a) 4
- b) 7
- c) 10
- d) 13

Q5: In one of the most famous moments in baseball history, Carl Hubbell struck out five consecutive future Hall of Famers in the 1934 All-Star Game at the Polo Grounds: Babe Ruth, Lou Gehrig, Jimmie Foxx, Al Simmons and Joe Cronin. Hubbell was a nine-time All-Star, two-time Most Valuable Player, and a world champion. What is the number retired by the Giants in honor of Carl Hubbell?
- a) 9
- b) 11
- c) 13
- d) 15

Q6: Juan Marichal is the most decorated pitcher in San Francisco Giants history. From 1958-2017, no pitcher had more wins, complete games, shutouts, innings or strikeouts for the Giants than did Marichal. He was inducted into the Hall of Fame in 1983. What is the number retired by the Giants in honor of Juan Marichal?
- a) 27
- b) 37
- c) 47
- d) 57

Q7: Gaylord Perry won 134 games for the Giants from 1962-71. Only two pitchers in the National League won more games during that stretch: Juan Marichal and Bob Gibson. Perry won 21 games in 1966 and 23 in 1970 as part of six consecutive 15-win seasons. He was inducted into the Hall of Fame in 1991. What is the number retired by the Giants in honor of

Gaylord Perry?
- a) 26
- b) 36
- c) 46
- d) 56

Q8: Willie McCovey was a three-time home run champion known for his prodigious bombs. Willie Mays once said, "He [McCovey] could hit a ball farther than anyone I ever played with." McCovey played parts of 19 seasons during two stints with the Giants, and was inducted into the Hall of Fame in 1986. What is the number retired by the Giants in honor of Willie McCovey?
- a) 24
- b) 34
- c) 44
- d) 54

Q9: In his first season with the club, Barry Bonds won two-thirds of the Triple Crown with a league-best 46 home runs and 123 RBIs. Bonds would go on to rewrite the record books during his 15 seasons with the Giants. What jersey number did Barry Bonds wear for the San Francisco Giants?
- a) 5
- b) 15
- c) 20
- d) 25

Q10: Will Clark was a standout Olympian in 1984 and later he won the Golden Spikes Award as the best amateur player in the country. Known as "The Thrill," Clark was a five-time All-Star during eight seasons with the Giants. What jersey number did Will Clark wear for the San Francisco Giants?
- a) 2
- b) 12
- c) 22
- d) 32

TOP OF THE FIRST—ANSWER KEY

1: c. 372.

2: b. 10.

3: a. 3.

4: a. 4.

5: b. 11.

6: a. 27.

7: b. 36.

8: c. 44.

9: d. 25.

10: c. 22.

BOTTOM OF THE FIRST

Q11: Hall of Fame legend Monte Irvin was a baseball and civil rights pioneer alongside Jackie Robinson and many other great Negro Leagues stars. He played 10 seasons with the Newark Eagles before he joined the Giants for seven seasons from 1949-55. His talent on the field is well-documented and the reason he made it to Cooperstown, but his class act as a human being is the reason his legacy not only endures but also continues to grow in significance. What is the number retired by the Giants in honor of Monte Irvin?
 a) 16
 b) 18
 c) 20
 d) 22

Q12: Willie Mays is the reason you hear so much about "five-tool" players. Not only was he capable of doing everything on the field, but also he did everything exceptionally well. Hall of Fame legend and a member of the All-Century Team ... Mays is quite simply the greatest baseball player in history. What is the number retired by the Giants in honor of Willie Mays?
 a) 21
 b) 24
 c) 27
 d) 30

Q13: Orlando Cepeda made his major-league debut on April 15, 1958, vs. the Los Angeles Dodgers—and he wasted no time endearing himself to the home crowd. Cepeda hit a fifth-inning home run to spark an 8-0 beat down of the Giants' most hated rival. Cepeda was an All-Star in six consecutive seasons from 1959-64, and he was inducted into the Hall of Fame in 1999. What is the number retired by the Giants in honor of Orlando Cepeda?
 a) 28
 b) 29
 c) 30
 d) 31

Q14: In seven seasons from 1968-74, Bobby Bonds hit 11 leadoff home

runs on the road … and another 17 home runs leading off the bottom of the first inning at home. Both numbers are franchise records. For good measure he also had five walk-off home runs for the Giants—the most of any player during Bonds' time with the club. What jersey number did Bobby Bonds wear for the San Francisco Giants?
- a) 5
- b) 15
- c) 20
- d) 25

Q15: Matt Williams was on pace for historic power numbers with 43 home runs and 96 RBIs in just 112 games in 1994 … but then the work stoppage happened, and killed the season. All total, Williams hit an impressive 247 home runs in parts of 10 seasons with the club. In fact, during his tenure in San Francisco, no other player was even close to his long ball total. Will Clark had the second most bombs during that time with 165. Williams wore a #60 jersey and a #10 jersey during call-ups in 1987 and 1988. What jersey number did Matt Williams wear for the San Francisco Giants from 1989-96?
- a) 6
- b) 9
- c) 12
- d) 15

Q16: Matt Cain won 104 games for the San Francisco Giants from 2005-17. He was also a big part of the Giants' postseason success in 2010, when he made three starts without allowing an earned run on the way to a world championship. Accidents and injuries derailed his career from 2014 onward, but he retired after 2017 as one of just seven pitchers to win 100 games in San Francisco. Cain wore #43 during his initial 2005 call-up. From 2006-17, what jersey number did Matt Cain wear for the Giants?
- a) 16
- b) 17
- c) 18
- d) 19

Q17: Kirk Rueter was acquired by the Giants in a 1996 trade deadline deal. He was a consistent presence in the rotation for the better part of a decade,

and when he left the game in 2005, his 105 wins were the most in San Francisco Giants history for a lefty. Rueter initially wore #42 when he joined the club in 1996—but then all of major-league baseball retired #42 in honor of Jackie Robinson, so Rueter wore #45 instead. He finally settled on one number for the rest of his tenure with the club. What jersey number did Kirk Rueter wear for the Giants from 1998-2005?
- a) 46
- b) 47
- c) 48
- d) 49

Q18: Jeff Kent had six prolific seasons with the Giants from 1997-2002. Only five second basemen in all of baseball had 100-plus home runs in that timeframe. Kent led them all with 175. He batted .297 with 247 doubles and 689 RBIs. Again, numbers that no other second baseman from either league came close to achieving. What jersey number did Jeff Kent wear for the Giants?
- a) 2
- b) 11
- c) 12
- d) 21

Q19: The Giants drafted Robby Thompson out of the University of Florida in 1983, and the second baseman made his big-league debut in 1986. Thompson played 149 games in his rookie season and led the club with 149 hits. He placed second in league Rookie of the Year balloting. For the better part of a decade he was a steady presence in the Giants lineup, and he would finish his career with 1,304 games—easily the most in San Francisco Giants history for a second baseman. What jersey number did Robby Thompson wear for the Giants?
- a) 3
- b) 4
- c) 5
- d) 6

Q20: Only nine players have hit 150 home runs for the San Francisco Giants. Jack Clark is eighth on that list with 163. The powerful outfielder/first baseman was a high school draft pick by the Giants in 1973.

He made his big-league debut just two years later and very quickly became one of the game's most-feared sluggers. He never posted truly prolific numbers, but for sure he gave pause to every opposing pitcher. Clark wore #15 as a rookie. What jersey number did Jack Clark wear for the Giants from 1977-84?

    a) 22
    b) 23
    c) 24
    d) 25

BOTTOM OF THE FIRST—ANSWER KEY

11: c. 20.

12: b. 24.

13: c. 30.

14: d. 25.

15: b. 9.

16: c. 18.

17: a. 46.

18: d. 21.

19: d. 6.

20: a. 22.

I feel fortunate that I had my one moment in the sun. It's nice to be remembered.

                                                            Bobby Thomson

2

You don't have to be a Giants fan to know about "The shot heard 'round the world." As a matter of fact you might not even have to be a real baseball fan to have a passable understanding of Bobby Thomson's famous home run. But some may forget all that had to happen for Ralph Branca to hurl that fateful pitch.

On August 11th, the Giants had just been swept by the hated Brooklyn Dodgers. They limped into their next game against Philadelphia and promptly got shutout. Four losses in a row and the Giants' playoff hopes appeared all but over as Leo Durocher's crew had fallen behind the Dodgers by 13 games. It made sense; after all, this is the club that started the season with just two wins in its first 14 tries.

Then a strange thing happened.

The Giants started winning, and winning, and winning, reeling of 16 straight victories and shrinking the Dodgers' lead to just five games. The Dodgers weren't willing to simply throw in the towel and let the Giants complete the amazing comeback. On September 21st the Giants still trailed by four games despite keeping a torrid pace.

Maybe the pressure started to crack the mighty Dodgers because they went 4-6 in their final 10 games. The Giants won their final seven games in September to force a playoff for the NL Pennant. It was a miracle that the Giants were in the position that they were in, and then they won the first game. Brooklyn bounced back with a 10-0 shellacking in game two, and this set the scene for Bobby Thomson to etch his name in history.

The game was something like a microcosm of the final seven weeks of the season. The Dodgers gained an early lead behind Hall of Famer Don Newcombe, 1-0. The Giants tied it in the seventh on a sac fly by Bobby Thomson.

Then it seemed that the comeback was over as Brooklyn answered with three runs in the top of the eighth. The score remained at 4-1 until the bottom of the ninth. Singles by Al Dark and Don Mueller gave the Giants hope, but it was dampened when Monte Irvin popped out to first.

With runners on first and third, Whitey Lockman fouled off Newcombe's first offering before slapping a double. The score was 4-2 with runners on second and third. The divided crowd was restless with anticipation. Ralph Branca replaced Newcombe. His first pitch was a called strike. Bobby Thomson ripped the second pitch into the left field seats and the Polo Grounds went bonkers. We now know it as the shot heard 'round the world, and it capped one of the most amazing comebacks in baseball history.

The Giants had done it.

From 13 games back in August to three runs down in the bottom of the ninth to quite possibly the most famous home run of all-time.

…

It's time for "Baseball Quotes" as the trivia continues here in the second inning … do you know which Giants these words were spoken about?

TOP OF THE SECOND

Q21: Hall of Fame manager Connie Mack once said of this pitcher: "He had knowledge, judgment, perfect control and form. It was wonderful to watch him pitch … when he wasn't pitching against you."
   a) Carl Hubbell
   b) Christy Mathewson
   c) Amos Rusie
   d) Tim Keefe

Q22: Christy Mathewson once said of this Giants legend: "He doesn't know what fear is."
   a) Bill Terry
   b) Mel Ott
   c) Carl Hubbell
   d) John McGraw

Q23: Dizzy Dean once said of this Giants legend: "He once hit a ball between my legs so hard, that my center fielder caught it on the fly backing up against the wall."
   a) Mel Ott
   b) Bill Terry
   c) Fred Lindstrom
   d) Lefty O'Doul

Q24: Hall of Fame manager Leo Durocher once said of this Giants legend: "I never knew a baseball player who was so universally loved. Why even when he was playing against the Dodgers at Ebbets Field, he would be cheered … and there are no more rabid fans than in Brooklyn."
   a) Fred Lindstrom
   b) Carl Hubbell
   c) Mel Ott
   d) Christy Mathewson

Q25: Hall of Fame second baseman Billy Herman once said of this pitcher: "He could throw strikes at midnight. I never saw another pitcher who could so fascinate the opposition the way [he] did."

a) Christy Mathewson
b) Juan Marichal
c) Carl Hubbell
d) Gaylord Perry

Q26: Bowie Kuhn, who spent 15 years as Commissioner of Major League Baseball, said of this player: "If they ever decide to start the Hall of Fame all over and place decency above all else, [he] would be the first man in."
a) Monte Irvin
b) Christy Mathewson
c) Willie Mays
d) Orlando Cepeda

Q27: Bill Rigney, a former player and long-time manager, once said of this player: "As a batter, his only weakness is a wild pitch."
a) Willie McCovey
b) Barry Bonds
c) Willie Mays
d) Orlando Cepeda

Q28: This legend's love for the game is evident in his words: "The trouble with baseball is that it is not played the year round."
a) Juan Marichal
b) Willie Mays
c) Monte Irvin
d) Gaylord Perry

Q29: Hall of Fame manager Sparky Anderson said of this slugger: "If you pitch to him, he'll ruin baseball. He'd hit 80 home runs."
a) Willie Mays
b) Willie McCovey
c) Bobby Bonds
d) Barry Bonds

Q30: Hall of Fame shortstop Ozzie Smith said of this all-time great: "Until I played at Candlestick, I never realized how great [he] must have been. My God, what would he have done in a real ballpark?
a) Willie McCovey

b) Willie Mays
c) Orlando Cepeda
d) Bobby Bonds

TOP OF THE SECOND—ANSWER KEY

21: b. Christy Mathewson.

22: d. John McGraw.

23: b. Bill Terry.

24: c. Mel Ott.

25: c. Carl Hubbell.

26: a. Monte Irvin.

27: c. Willie Mays.

28: d. Gaylord Perry.

29: b. Willie McCovey.

30: b. Willie Mays.

BOTTOM OF THE SECOND

Q31: This Hall of Fame legend once said: "The game of ball is only fun for me when I'm out in front and winning."
   a) John McGraw
   b) Mel Ott
   c) Carl Hubbell
   d) Bill Terry

Q32: Lee Allen, who was a noted sportswriter and baseball historian, once said of this legend: "He has often been misunderstood, and what passed for coldness has merely been an impatience with stupid questions."
   a) John McGraw
   b) Mel Ott
   c) Carl Hubbell
   d) Bill Terry

Q33: Bobby Thomson hit the "shot heard 'round the world" to beat the Dodgers and win the pennant in 1951 … but Thomson gave credit to this teammate for the club's success that year: "I've been giving talks since my playing career ended and I always said the same thing: we would not have made that huge comeback in 1951 and won the pennant at the end, if it weren't for [him]."
   a) Willie Mays
   b) Hank Thompson
   c) Monte Irvin
   d) Eddie Stanky

Q34: Giants manager Alvin Dark once said of this pitcher: "Put your club a run ahead in the later innings, and [he] is the greatest pitcher I ever saw."
   a) Carl Hubbell
   b) Vida Blue
   c) Juan Marichal
   d) Gaylord Perry

Q35: This slugger was so good at the plate that Willie Mays said, "He's annoying every pitcher in the league."

a) Orlando Cepeda
b) Willie McCovey
c) Bobby Bonds
d) Barry Bonds

Q36: This player was asked what would improve Candlestick Park. His pithy, snarky, and perfect reply: "Dynamite."
a) Jack Clark
b) Dusty Baker
c) Roger Craig
d) Felipe Alou

Q37: This player famously said: "It's great to be young and a Giant."
a) Mel Ott
b) Bill Terry
c) Larry Doyle
d) Frankie Frisch

Q38: This member of the Giants, upon winning the 2010 World Series, said: "This buried a lot of bones—'62, '89, 2002. This group deserved it, faithful from the beginning. We're proud and humbled by the achievement."
a) Bruce Bochy
b) Brian Sabean
c) Fred Stanley
d) John Barr

Q39: It's not arrogance, just a fact. This player once said: "I was born to hit a baseball. I can hit a baseball."
a) Orlando Cepeda
b) Jack Clark
c) Barry Bonds
d) Willie McCovey

Q40: Bobby Thomson's "shot heard 'round the world" elicited this play call: "The Giants win the pennant! The Giants win the pennant! The Giants win the pennant! The Giants win the pennant!" It never gets old. Who called Bobby Thomson's historic home run?

a) Ernie Harwell
b) Bob DeLaney
c) Maury Farrell
d) Russ Hodges

BOTTOM OF THE SECOND—ANSWER KEY

31: a. John McGraw.

32: d. Bill Terry.

33: c. Monte Irvin.

34: c. Juan Marichal.

35: a. Orlando Cepeda.

36: a. Jack Clark.

37: c. Larry Doyle.

38: b. Brian Sabean.

39: c. Barry Bonds.

40: d. Russ Hodges.

Some will win, some will lose
Some are born to sing the blues
Oh the movie never ends
It goes on and on and on and on

Strangers waiting
Up and down the boulevard
Their shadows searchin' in the night

Streetlight, people
Livin' just to find emotion
Hidin' somewhere in the night

Don't stop believin'
Hold on to that feelin'
Streetlight, people, oh oh oh

Don't stop believin'
Hold on to that feelin'
Streetlight, people, oh oh oh

Don't stop!

Steve Perry, Jonathan Cain, Neal Schon
Journey, "Don't Stop Believin'"

3

SAN FRANCISCO. October 27, 1977. Steve Perry made his public debut as the lead man for Journey and was met with mixed reviews. His style was different than the band's previous sound.

In time, however, he won over the fans.

Just four years later, Journey released what is arguably their most famous single: "Don't Stop Believin'".

For diehard Giants fans, it was a difficult stretch. It was hard to keep the faith.

"Don't Stop Believin'"?

Maybe impossible.

Since the move to San Francisco in 1958 the club had only made two postseason appearances. The first was the absolutely amazing 1962 team that came oh so close to beating the Yankees to claim the title. The second came nine years later when the 1971 edition lost the National League Championship Series to the Pirates, three games to one.

The '70s, and much of the '80s, were about as bleak as they come. In 1985 the club lost 100 games and was 33 games out of first place, and this was on the heels of a season in which they mustered only 66 wins. As a matter of fact, from 1972 to 1986 the Giants finished no higher than 3rd in the NL West.

As the Giants' woes continued, Steve Perry and Journey were just hitting their stride. One of Perry's first contributions to the band was the ballad "Lights"—a song that was originally written about Los Angeles but later changed to San Francisco, the city that Perry loved. It was not long after that when the band exploded with songs like "Who's Cryin' Now", "Open Arms", and "Don't Stop Believing".

After the abysmal stretch in the '70s and '80s and near the end of Journey's huge commercial success, the Giants began to turn it around, making it to the postseason six times including the heartbreaking World Series Game 7 loss to the Angels in 2002.

Fast-forward to October 27, 2010, exactly 33 years after Steve Perry took the stage with Journey. It's Game 1 of the 2010 World Series against the upstart Texas Rangers. With "Don't Stop Believing" now the unofficial song of the Giants, the Rangers struck early with single runs in the first and second innings. Surely many of those in the crowd wondered if this would be another disappointment for their beloved Giants. But two runs in the third and six more in the bottom of the fifth helped to quell those fears.

The Giants rolled to an 11-7 victory and they didn't stop there. Clinging to a 2-0 lead in the bottom of the eighth in Game 2, Steve Perry led the crowd in the singing of "Lights" and the Giants promptly put a seven-spot on the board to roll to a 9-0 victory. The club went on to claim the World Series title in five games and there was reason to celebrate in San Francisco.

The singing of "Don't Stop Believing" (when the Giants are down) and "Lights" (when the Giants are up), has become one of the coolest traditions in baseball. And it's been great for Steve Perry as well, as he's said, "I can't put into words what the Giants have done for me emotionally. It's beyond words. In a lot of ways, they've saved me and they've gotten me back into music, to be perfectly honest with you. They touched me in a way that made me excited about music again."

The Giants claimed the title again in 2012 and 2014.

Those lean years are all but forgotten.

And as Giants fans, young and old, will now tell you, "Don't stop believing!"

...

In the third inning it's all about "Franchise Records" … do you know which Giants achieved these historic feats?

TOP OF THE THIRD

Q41: Hall of Fame pitcher Jack Chesbro set a major-league record for the modern era when he won 41 games for the 1904 New York Yankees. A member of the New York Giants set a franchise and modern era NL record with a 37-win season. Who holds this untouchable record?
　a) Carl Hubbell
　b) Christy Mathewson
　c) Amos Rusie
　d) Tim Keefe

Q42: Only seven players in major-league history had 250 hits in a single-season. One of those seven did it for the Giants. Who set franchise records with 254 hits and a .401 average for the New York Giants?
　a) Fred Lindstrom
　b) Frankie Frisch
　c) Rogers Hornsby
　d) Bill Terry

Q43: From 1958-2017, only three players had 200 hits in a single-season for the San Francisco Giants. Who holds the franchise record with 208 hits in a season?
　a) Willie Mays
　b) Rich Aurilia
　c) Bobby Bonds
　d) Barry Bonds

Q44: Christy Mathewson had a 16-strikeout game in 1904. No Giants pitcher has ever eclipsed that mark, though several have come close—most notably Madison Bumgarner, who had three 14-strikeout games in 2015-16 alone—and one actually tied it. Who is the only other pitcher in franchise history to record 16 strikeouts in one game?
　a) Tim Lincecum
　b) Gaylord Perry
　c) Jason Schmidt
　d) John Montefusco

Q45: In 1944, first baseman Phil Weintraub had a game vs. Brooklyn with two doubles, a triple, home run, five runs scored, and 11 RBIs. The Giants won 26-8 in one of the most lopsided games in Giants-Dodgers rivalry history. Weintraub's 11 RBIs is a franchise record for all eras. The highest single-game total for the San Francisco Giants is eight. Which two players share this record?
  a) Barry Bonds/Jeff Kent
  b) Bobby Bonds/Hunter Pence
  c) Willie Mays/Orlando Cepeda
  d) Jarrett Parker/Marco Scutaro

Q46: In 1897, third baseman Bill Joyce had four triples in a game for the New York Giants. From 1958-2017, the San Francisco Giants single-game record for triples is three. Who had five hits and three triples in a game vs. the Philadelphia Phillies?
  a) Bobby Bonds
  b) Barry Bonds
  c) Willie Mays
  d) Hunter Pence

Q47: Four players in San Francisco Giants history have hit more than 25 career home runs vs. the Los Angeles Dodgers: Barry Bonds, Matt Williams, Willie Mays, and Willie McCovey. Which player hit a franchise record 56 bombs against the Giants most-hated rival?
  a) Barry Bonds
  b) Matt Williams
  c) Willie Mays
  d) Willie McCovey

Q48: Among players with at least 35 games and 125 at-bats, who has the highest career batting average vs. the Dodgers?
  a) Brett Butler
  b) Bobby Murcer
  c) Will Clark
  d) Buster Posey

Q49: Willie Mays is the only player in franchise history to hit double-digit home runs vs. the Dodgers in a single-season. He did it in 1958, when he

batted .483 with 43 hits, 27 runs, and 32 RBIs in just 21 games. How many home runs did Willie Mays hit vs. Los Angeles in 1958?
- a) 10
- b) 11
- c) 12
- d) 13

Q50: George Davis hit safely in a franchise record 33 consecutive games in 1893 … as for the modern era, the longest hitting streak in San Francisco Giants history is 26 games. Who holds this impressive record?
- a) Buster Posey
- b) Jack Clark
- c) Al Dark
- d) Randy Winn

TOP OF THE THIRD—ANSWER KEY

41: b. Christy Mathewson.

42: d. Bill Terry.

43: a. Willie Mays.

44: c. Jason Schmidt.

45: c. Willie Mays/Orlando Cepeda.

46: c. Willie Mays.

47: c. Willie Mays.

48: b. Bobby Murcer.

49: c. 12.

50: b. Jack Clark.

BOTTOM OF THE THIRD

Q51: Among his many accomplishments, John McGraw won 2,763 games—the second highest total in history behind Connie Mack—and was the first manager in major-league history to win four consecutive pennants. His fiery demeanor also came into play more than a few times. McGraw was ejected more than any manager in history until, decades later, Atlanta's Bobby Cox finally surpassed this dubious mark. How many times was John McGraw ejected during his managerial career?
   a) 101
   b) 111
   c) 121
   d) 131

Q52: From 1958-2017, the Giants hit 133 walk-off home runs. In 1959, Jack Hiatt hit the first-ever walk-off grand slam for the club. Only two other players have ever repeated that feat: Bobby Bonds and Leon Wagner. Who hit a franchise record eight career walk-off home runs for the Giants?
   a) Will Clark
   b) Willie McCovey
   c) Bobby Bonds
   d) Barry Bonds

Q53: The Giants and Dodgers played 2,468 regular season games from 1890 through 2017. The Giants won 1,240 and lost 1,211. All those games, and only 27 pitchers in Giants history have won as many as 10 games against the Dodgers. The franchise record against the Giants most-hated rival is 37 wins and 10 shutouts. Who achieved these remarkable numbers?
   a) Juan Marichal
   b) Christy Mathewson
   c) Carl Hubbell
   d) Sal Maglie

Q54: The Giants claim eight batting titles from all eras of franchise history. The first two go back to the 1800s, and the next three were won with the modern era New York Giants. The San Francisco Giants also claim three batting titles from 1958-2017. Who set a San Francisco Giants franchise

record and won a batting title with his .370 average?
a) Willie Mays
b) Barry Bonds
c) Buster Posey
d) Jeff Kent

Q55: This player won the first modern era batting title in franchise history when he batted .320 in 1915. Who won this prestigious title?
a) Larry Doyle
b) George Burns
c) Fred Snodgrass
d) Fred Merkle

Q56: The Giants have been the home team for some of the best switch-hitters in baseball. In the San Francisco era of Giants baseball, who holds the franchise record for highest season average by a switch-hitter?
a) Ray Durham
b) Randy Winn
c) Chili Davis
d) Pablo Sandoval

Q57: And a follow-up to that last question … in the San Francisco era of Giants baseball, who holds the franchise record for most home runs in a season by a switch-hitter?
a) Ray Durham
b) Randy Winn
c) Chili Davis
d) Pablo Sandoval

Q58: Only one player in San Francisco Giants history has hit 30 home runs during his rookie season. Who is this exceptional talent?
a) Orlando Cepeda
b) Dave Kingman
c) Jim Ray Hart
d) Chili Davis

Q59: A .500 slugging percentage is a big deal. In fact, from 1958-2017, only 21 players achieved that mark for the Giants while also tallying enough at-bats to qualify among the league leaders. Barry Bonds had more such seasons than anyone (and he also had some seasons with a .500 slugging percentage but without enough at bats to qualify among the league leaders). What is the franchise record number of seasons in which Barry Bonds had a .500 slugging percentage?

    a) 8
    b) 9
    c) 10
    d) 11

Q60: And a follow-up to that last question … who are the only rookies in San Francisco Giants history to play 100 games *and* post a .500 slugging percentage?

    a) Bobby Bonds/Willie McCovey
    b) Matt Williams/Will Clark
    c) Jack Clark/Pablo Sandoval
    d) Buster Posey/Orlando Cepeda

BOTTOM OF THE THIRD—ANSWER KEY

51: d. 131.

52: d. Barry Bonds.

53: a. Juan Marichal.

54: b. Barry Bonds.

55: a. Larry Doyle.

56: d. Pablo Sandoval.

57: a. Ray Durham.

58: c. Jim Ray Hart.

59: d. 11.

60: d. Buster Posey/Orlando Cepeda.

We had a model, and we took it from place to place around the city and we showed balls landing in the water. It was great. People said, 'This is magical.'

Larry Baer

4

B.A.R.K. stands for Baseball Aquatic Retrieval Korp and it was the brainchild of one Father Guido Sarducci of *The Smothers Brothers* and *Saturday Night Live* fame.

We can't make this stuff up.

Back in the '90s, Don Novello (Father Guido) came to the Giants with the idea of having dogs chase home run balls that splashed into McCovey Cove. At first it was met with little enthusiasm, but after Pets In Need got involved the idea grew legs. It was decided that the splash hits would be donated to the organization and the Giants would offer up a $5,000 donation at the end of the season.

Six Portuguese Water Dogs were the chosen splash hit chasers and they were the perfect fit since they've been used for centuries to herd fish. They trained for their important duty, but they didn't make their debut until July 2000. Heading into the inaugural campaign at Pac Bell it seemed that baseballs would be flying into the cove on a regular basis with that enticing 309 sign down the right field line. But it quickly proved to not be so easy.

It was May 1st when Barry Bonds dug in against Yankee lefty Rich Rodriguez. He hammered a towering fly ball that launched into the San Francisco night and aimed for the water. The ball touched down with a splash and with no Portuguese Water Dogs in sight two boats raced for the bobbing treasure. The guy who got to the ball celebrated by popping open a bottle of champagne.

A little over a week later Bonds scored two splash hits against the Cards and it seemed that it would become a regular thing.

Not so much though.

Hitting a ball into the cove has proven to be much harder than expected. The most splashes in one season by the Giants was 11 in 2001.

Bonds launched nine of them with Felipe Crespo belting the other two. In both 2006 and 2013 the Giants only hit one ball into the water. Bonds was the only one to reach the water in 2006 and Pablo Sandoval held the 2013 honors.

According to physics professor David Kagan in an article at *Hardball Times*, despite the short distance down the right field line it still takes a 367 foot shot to reach the cove. Add just a ten degree angle and the ball has to travel 404 feet to get wet. Make it a twenty degree angle and it takes a 466 foot blast to reach the water!

The B.A.R.K. program was retired after a couple of seasons in part because the dogs just weren't getting enough action, but more importantly it became unsafe for them with all the boaters hoping to claim a unique souvenir.

…

The fourth inning is all about "October Baseball" … how much do you know about Giants in the postseason?

TOP OF THE FOURTH

Q61: The New York Giants won the 1905 World Series for the first modern era championship in franchise history. It was an unusual series vs. the Philadelphia Athletics in that all five games were shutouts. One pitcher led the way with three complete game shutouts for the Giants. Who was the star of the 1905 World Series?
  a) Red Ames
  b) Christy Mathewson
  c) Joe McGinnity
  d) Hooks Wiltse

Q62: Bobby Thomson's "shot heard 'round the world" is perhaps the most famous home run in major-league history. It was a pennant-winning blast to beat an archrival in a best-of-three playoff—and it was only made possible after the Giants torrid 50-12 finish to rally from 13 games back on August 11. Who was in the on-deck circle when Thomson hit his historic walk-off home run?
  a) Monte Irvin
  b) Willie Mays
  c) Hank Thompson
  d) Eddie Stanky

Q63: The 1969 Chicago Cubs spent 156 days in first place in the NL East but blew a nine-game lead in the season's final weeks and missed the postseason. No major-league team failed so epically again until the 2007 New York Mets (159 days in first). And then it happened to the Arizona Diamondbacks in 2008 (158 days in first), the Detroit Tigers in 2009 (165 days in first) … and back to the NL West in 2010. This team led the Giants by 6 1/2 games on August 25 and spent 147 days in first throughout the season … but a ten-game skid and a furious finish by San Francisco gave the Giants the division title. Which team collapsed in 2010 to pave the way for the Giants' postseason glory?
  a) Los Angeles Dodgers
  b) Colorado Rockies
  c) Arizona Diamondbacks

d) San Diego Padres

Q64: A lot of things need to go right for a club to win a division title and find success in the postseason. When your starting rotation boasts four guys who each make 33 starts … that counts as something going right. Matt Cain, Tim Lincecum, Barry Zito, and Jonathan Sanchez all made 33 starts and pitched 190-plus innings in 2010—plus, Madison Bumgarner joined the club at the end of June and won seven games in 18 starts—and the staff carried that success into October. Who started and won Game 5 of the World Series for his fourth victory of the postseason and the first world championship in San Francisco Giants history?
   a) Matt Cain
   b) Tim Lincecum
   c) Barry Zito
   d) Jonathan Sanchez

Q65: The longest postseason hitting streak in history is 17 games. It's been done twice, by Manny Ramirez and Derek Jeter. Through 2017, the longest postseason hitting streak in San Francisco Giants history is 14. Who holds this record?
   a) Marco Scutaro
   b) Hunter Pence
   c) Pablo Sandoval
   d) Cody Ross

Q66: From 1958-2017, only one player had a postseason walk-off home run for the Giants. It also won the pennant. Who won the 2014 NLCS with a Game 5 walk-off home run vs. Michael Wacha and the St. Louis Cardinals?
   a) Brandon Belt
   b) Travis Ishikawa
   c) Brandon Crawford
   d) Hunter Pence

Q67: The 2016 Giants won a wild card berth in the postseason despite blowing a franchise record 30 saves on the season. In the Wild Card Game, Madison Bumgarner pitched a complete game, four-hit shutout on the road vs. the New York Mets. The final score was 3-0. All three runs scored on

one swing of the bat in a dramatic ninth inning. Whose three-run home run won the 2016 Wild Card Game?
   a) Brandon Crawford
   b) Hunter Pence
   c) Joe Panik
   d) Conor Gillaspie

Q68: Madison Bumgarner also pitched a complete game, four-hit shutout on the road vs. the Pittsburgh Pirates in the 2014 Wild Card Game. All the offense he needed that night also came with one swing of the bat. Who hit a grand slam in the 2014 Wild Card Game that set the Giants on the path to World Series glory?
   a) Joe Panik
   b) Brandon Belt
   c) Pablo Sandoval
   d) Brandon Crawford

Q69: Only once in major-league history has a player been credited with a five-inning save in the postseason. He did it for the Giants. Who is this pitcher?
   a) Tim Lincecum
   b) Matt Cain
   c) Madison Bumgarner
   d) Jeremy Affeldt

Q70: The 2012 San Francisco Giants won a second World Series title in three years in historic fashion. Cincinnati had the Giants on the brink of elimination in the Division Series but couldn't get it done. St. Louis was one win away from the pennant in the Championship Series but couldn't close out the Giants. What is the record-tying number of consecutive elimination games that the Giants won during the 2012 postseason?
   a) 3
   b) 4
   c) 5
   d) 6

TOP OF THE FOURTH—ANSWER KEY

61: b. Christy Mathewson.

62: b. Willie Mays.

63: d. San Diego Padres.

64: b. Tim Lincecum.

65: c. Pablo Sandoval.

66: b. Travis Ishikawa.

67: d. Conor Gillaspie.

68: d. Brandon Crawford.

69: c. Madison Bumgarner (2014 World Series, Game 7).

70: d. 6.

BOTTOM OF THE FOURTH

Q71: Here's an exclusive group: through 2017, only 10 players in major-league history hit three home runs in a postseason game. One of them did it for the Giants. Who is this slugger?
   a) Barry Bonds
   b) Willie Mays
   c) Pablo Sandoval
   d) Jeff Kent

Q72: In the third week of August 2002, the Giants were 66-56 and four games behind the Dodgers for the NL wild card. A furious finish, however, set the stage for a dramatic October. The Giants won 29 games against just 10 losses the rest of the way to win the wild card by 3 1/2 games. In the NLDS, the Giants knocked off a heavily-favored Atlanta Braves thanks to clutch pitching and a dramatic bomb. On the pitching side … whose Game 5 victory made him the first Giants pitcher since Carl Hubbell in 1933 to win two games in the same postseason series?
   a) Kirk Rueter
   b) Livan Hernandez
   c) Russ Ortiz
   d) Jason Schmidt

Q73: As for the bomb … who singled and scored the first run of the deciding Game 5 in the 2002 Division Series vs. Atlanta, and then later added an opposite field solo home run that proved to be the winning run in the Giants 3-1 victory?
   a) J.T. Snow
   b) Rich Aurilia
   c) Barry Bonds
   d) Reggie Sanders

Q74: And speaking of bombs … the first-ever postseason Splash Hit came in the 2002 National League Championship Series. Who launched a home run into McCovey Cove against Cardinals lefty Chuck Finley?
   a) J.T. Snow
   b) Barry Bonds

c) Bill Mueller
d) Tony Torcato

Q75: In Game 4 of the 2002 NLCS vs. St. Louis, the Cardinals led 2-0 until J.T. Snow delivered a two-out, game-tying double in the sixth. With the go-ahead run on second, the Cardinals elected to intentionally walk Barry Bonds. Normally that's a smart move. On this night it backfired. Who followed the intentional walk to Bonds with a go-ahead home run that proved to be the game-winner?
a) Benito Santiago
b) Reggie Sanders
c) Bill Mueller
d) Rich Aurilia

Q76: The Giants led the 2002 NLCS three games to one when Cardinals ace Matt Morris took the mound for Game 5. The Giants had routed Morris in Game 1. However, Game 5 was a different story. Morris carried a shutout into the eighth and was still on the mound in the ninth with the scored tied 1-1. Morris retired the first two batters, but couldn't get the third out. David Bell and Shawon Dunston both singled, and the Cardinals brought lefty Steve Kline in from the bullpen. Kline threw exactly one pitch. Who singled and won the pennant with the very first postseason walk-off in San Francisco Giants history?
a) J.T. Snow
b) Tom Goodwin
c) Benito Santiago
d) Kenny Lofton

Q77: In the 2002 postseason, the Giants had three different players with 16 or more RBIs. To put that into perspective, through 2017, Buster Posey is the franchise leader with 23 *career* postseason RBIs ... and that's for a guy who has won three world championships. Who set a franchise record with 17 RBIs during the 2002 postseason?
a) Jeff Kent
b) Barry Bonds
c) Rich Aurilia
d) Benito Santiago

Q78: For the first time in major-league history, the 2002 World Series featured two teams that were both wild cards. San Francisco and Anaheim played a back-and-forth series that was more sandlot slugfest than anything else. With the series tied two games apiece … who powered the Giants to a 16-4 Game 5 victory—and one win from a world championship—with four runs, two home runs, and four RBIs?
  a) Jeff Kent
  b) Barry Bonds
  c) Rich Aurilia
  d) Benito Santiago

Q79: The Giants had a 5-0 lead in Game 6 of the 2002 World Series. Just eight outs away from a world championship, the unthinkable happened. Scott Spiezio hit a three-run home run in the seventh inning, and then the series MVP hit a two-run double in the eighth to rally Anaheim to a 6-5 victory. Anaheim would go on to win Game 7 behind the pitching of John Lackey, 4-1. Who was the 2002 World Series MVP for the Anaheim Angels?
  a) Garret Anderson
  b) Darin Erstad
  c) Troy Glaus
  d) Tim Salmon

Q80: Will Clark, Buster Posey, and Brandon Crawford all had memorable postseason grand slams for the Giants … but, who is the only player in franchise history to hit a grand slam in the World Series?
  a) Chuck Hiller
  b) Jim Davenport
  c) Tom Haller
  d) Felipe Alou

BOTTOM OF THE FOURTH—ANSWER KEY

71: c. Pablo Sandoval (2012 World Series, Game 1).

72: c. Russ Ortiz.

73: c. Barry Bonds.

74: b. Barry Bonds.

75: a. Benito Santiago.

76: d. Kenny Lofton.

77: c. Rich Aurilia.

78: a. Jeff Kent.

79: c. Troy Glaus.

80: a. Chuck Hiller (1962 World Series, Game 4).

It would almost be easier for Giants fans if there were a Bill Buckner to blame.

Josh Rawitch

5

WHEN Kenny Lofton flew out to center field against Anaheim's Troy Percival it brought an end to one of the most exciting World Series in recent memory. Unfortunately the Giants had come up one game short ... again.

The 2002 campaign had been marked with solid pitching (every regular starter had at least 12 wins) and powered by the bats of Barry Bonds and Jeff Kent. Despite the Game 7 loss, hopes were high heading into the 2003 season.

Then came massive turnover.

Jeff Kent left for Houston, David Bell, Kenny Lofton, and Reggie Sanders were gone as well. Dusty Baker was replaced with Felipe Alou. Closer Robb Nen had to retire due to a shoulder injury. Livan Hernandez and Russ Ortiz no longer donned the orange and black either.

But the club won 13 of 14 to begin 2013, and any concern from all the turnover was quickly alleviated. The Giants took hold of first place and never relinquished it. Jason Schmidt became the go-to guy on the mound and newly acquired position players Marquis Grissom and Jose Cruz Jr. filled in nicely for the departed 2002 bunch.

It was a season filled with seven winning streaks of at least five games, the longest being nine straight in July. Once again, the Giants faithful were filled with optimism heading into the NL Division Series against the Marlins, a team the club had beaten five out of six times during the regular season.

After a stellar pitching performance by Jason Schmidt in Game 1 all was right in the world. Game 2 saw the Giants jump out to a four-run lead, and then the wheels fell off. The Marlins rallied for the win, and then came from one run down in the 11th to win Game 3.

Hopes for that elusive World Series title slipped away in Game 4 when the Marlins ended the Giants season with another one-run victory on their way to winning the World Series.

The Giants had put together two great seasons, but frustration was high. Giants fans wondered if a title would ever come to San Francisco.

The title did come, of course.

And now success is ubiquitous to the Giants.

...

The fifth inning is all about "The Sluggers" ... guys who can hit the ball a mile. How much do you know about these all-time greats?

TOP OF THE FIFTH

Q81: Barry Bonds hit 30 home runs a franchise record 12 times. All total the Giants had 48 such seasons by 13 different players from 1958-2017. Which means, incredibly, that 25% of the Giants' 30-homer seasons belong to Barry Bonds. However, one of the other players in the 30-homer club accomplished something that no one else—not even Bonds—has done in San Francisco. Who is the only player in San Francisco Giants history with 30 home runs *and* 200 hits in the same season?
 a) Matt Williams
 b) Willie McCovey
 c) Rich Aurilia
 d) Jeff Kent

Q82: Barry Bonds is at the top of baseball's all-time home run list with 762, but he isn't the only slugger to suit it up for the Giants. Not by a long shot. In fact, the list of baseball's all-time home run leaders is filled with Giants … and one of them was the first NL player in history to reach 500 home runs. Who achieved this historic milestone?
 a) Willie McCovey
 b) Willie Mays
 c) Mel Ott
 d) Orlando Cepeda

Q83: Bill Duggleby was a pitcher for the Philadelphia Phillies in 1898 when he became the first-ever rookie to hit a grand slam in his major-league debut. For decades, Duggleby had the distinction of being the only player to ever accomplish that feat … until this slugger came along. Who was the first modern era player to hit a grand slam—against the Dodgers, no less— during his major-league debut?
 a) Bobby Bonds
 b) Matt Williams
 c) Pedro Feliz
 d) Jack Clark

Q84: Five players in franchise history have hit three grand slams in a single-season—most recently Jeff Kent, in 1997—but who hit a record 16 career

grand slams?
    a) Willie McCovey
    b) Bobby Bonds
    c) Barry Bonds
    d) Willie Mays

Q85: This player hit 18 home runs in only 96 games for the 2010 Giants after being released by Tampa Bay earlier in the season. His home run total is the highest in franchise history for a player who began the season with another team. Who is this slugger?
    a) Aubrey Huff
    b) Pat Burrell
    c) Jose Guillen
    d) Cody Ross

Q86: Only 11 players have hit 10 home runs in a single month for the San Francisco Giants. However, those 11 players have achieved this feat a combined *51 times* … including *20* for Barry Bonds and *11* for Willie Mays. After Bonds and Mays, the next highest total is seven. Who hit 10 home runs in a month seven times in his career?
    a) Willie McCovey
    b) Kevin Mitchell
    c) Jeff Kent
    d) Matt Williams

Q87: Ken Henderson was a switch-hitting outfielder with the Giants from 1965-72. He had just 61 home runs in eight seasons … but he hit 10 of them in August 1972 to become the first switch-hitter in franchise history with ten bombs in one month. Through 2017, who is the only other switch-hitter with a 10-homer month for the San Francisco Giants?
    a) Chili Davis
    b) Randy Winn
    c) Pablo Sandoval
    d) Ray Durham

Q88: From 1958-2017, the Giants had 394 walk-off hits. The opponent the Giants punished the most was the Los Angeles Dodgers: 41 times. And the slugger who had more walk-off hits than any other player?

a) Barry Bonds
b) Willie Mays
c) Will Clark
d) Willie McCovey

Q89: And just for fun … the Giants also had 18 walk-off walks from 1958-2017. That's right. Bases loaded. Game tied. And a true walk-off. Who is the only player in franchise history with two walk-off walks?
a) Aaron Rowand
b) Buster Posey
c) Jeff Kent
d) Marquis Grissom

Q90: The four players with the most intentional walks in franchise history are Barry Bonds (575), Willie McCovey (235), Willie Mays (139), and Will Clark (112). Who is the only slugger in team history to draw an intentional walk with the bases loaded?
a) Barry Bonds
b) Willie McCovey
c) Willie Mays
d) Will Clark

TOP OF THE FIFTH—ANSWER KEY

81: c. Rich Aurilia.

82: c. Mel Ott.

83: a. Bobby Bonds.

84: a. Willie McCovey.

85: b. Pat Burrell.

86: d. Matt Williams.

87: b. Randy Winn.

88: a. Barry Bonds.

89: c. Jeff Kent.

90: a. Barry Bonds.

BOTTOM OF THE FIFTH

Q91: Barry Bonds had four seasons with 150-plus walks—all four with the Giants. Babe Ruth and Ted Williams are the only other players in major-league history with multiple seasons of 150 walks. In 2004, Bonds struck out only 41 times all year but hit 45 home runs. He also set major-league records for walks and intentional walks. Bonds was put on intentionally 120 times. What is the absolutely insane number of times Bonds walked on the season?
  a) 202
  b) 212
  c) 222
  d) 232

Q92: Only eight players in San Francisco Giants history had double-digits in home runs, doubles, triples, and stolen bases in a single-season. Willie Mays did it twice. The most recent player to achieve this feat did so in 2014 … who is he?
  a) Hunter Pence
  b) Angel Pagan
  c) Brandon Crawford
  d) Brandon Hicks

Q93: From 1958-2017, the Giants had 16 different players hit 10 or more triples in a single-season. For 56 years Willie Mays was the only player with two such seasons. Brandon Crawford did it for the second time in 2016 and if he can do it again he'll leapfrog a legend in the record books—which isn't something that happens very often. However, neither Mays nor Crawford holds the single-season record for triples. Who had 15 in one season for a franchise record?
  a) Melky Cabrera
  b) Hunter Pence
  c) Bobby Bonds
  d) Angel Pagan

Q94: Only six players in San Francisco Giants history had a single-season with 100 RBIs, 100 runs, a .300 average, and a .500 slugging percentage.

Willie Mays was the first to do so, in 1959. Jeff Kent was the most recent, in 2002. But who had a franchise record seven such seasons for the Giants?
   a) Orlando Cepeda
   b) Willie McCovey
   c) Willie Mays
   d) Barry Bonds

Q95: In San Francisco Giants history, the longest RBI streak is 10 games. It's been done twice. Which players had at least one RBI in 10 consecutive games?
   a) Barry Bonds/Willie McCovey
   b) Pablo Sandoval/Will Clark
   c) Willie Mays/Orlando Cepeda
   d) Jeff Kent/Matt Williams

Q96: In July 2004, Barry Bonds had an eight-game streak in which he reached base at least three times per game ... and then two months later he did it again. Until Bonds, only one player in franchise history had ever reached base three times or more in eight consecutive games. In fact, the second longest streak in club history is five games. Who had an eight-game streak with three or more times on base in 1975?
   a) Gary Matthews
   b) Bobby Murcer
   c) Steve Ontiveros
   d) Chris Speier

Q97: Who is the youngest player in San Francisco Giants history—at 20 years, 229 days—to hit two home runs in one game?
   a) Ken Henderson
   b) Orlando Cepeda
   c) Willie McCovey
   d) Matt Williams

Q98: Barry Bonds dominated NL pitching for 15 years with the Giants. He hit 586 home runs for the club, which arguably makes him one of the best free agent signings in major-league history. Bonds last played in 2007. Who has hit the most home runs for the Giants in the post-Barry Bonds era? A side note ... with 17 and counting, pitcher Madison Bumgarner currently

ranks 17th out of 95 players to homer for the Giants since 2008 …
   a) Buster Posey
   b) Pablo Sandoval
   c) Brandon Belt
   d) Hunter Pence

Q99: Buster Posey is only the second catcher in San Francisco Giants history to hit 100 career home runs. Who was the first?
   a) Tom Haller
   b) Bob Brenly
   c) Dick Dietz
   d) Bengie Molina

Q100: The Giants have hit more than 400 home runs at Dodger Stadium. Which slugger hit a franchise record 25 long balls at the home of the Giants' biggest rival?
   a) Darrell Evans
   b) Jack Clark
   c) Barry Bonds
   d) Matt Williams

BOTTOM OF THE FIFTH—ANSWER KEY

91: d. 232.

92: a. Hunter Pence.

93: d. Angel Pagan.

94: d. Barry Bonds.

95: d. Jeff Kent/Matt Williams.

96: b. Bobby Murcer.

97: b. Orlando Cepeda.

98: a. Buster Posey (130, and counting).

99: a. Tom Haller.

100: c. Barry Bonds.

If you placed all the pitchers in the history of the game behind a transparent curtain, where only a silhouette was visible, Juan's motion would be the easiest to identify. He brought to the mound beauty, individuality and class.

Bob Stevens

6

ON August 16, 2015, the San Francisco Giants played host to the Washington Nationals, and Giants Hall of Famer Juan Marichal was on hand. He still pulls for his Giants, but on this day he was at AT&T Park because 20,000 lucky fans were given a replica of his statue.

It was almost exactly ten years earlier, May 21, 2005, when Juan Marichal's statue was dedicated in Lefty O'Doul Plaza just outside of the park. The massive statue weighs a ton and replicates Marichal's signature delivery with his left leg pointed to the sky. It was a major feat by sculptor William Behrends, who also did the statues for Willie Mays, Willie McCovey, and Orlando Cepeda. Behrends, a diehard Giants fan, said, "Marichal was quite an athlete. Just that delivery was quite an athletic feat. That sculpture sits on one leg, so it has to be really strong."

It is strong.

Just like Marichal's incredible pitching credentials. In 471 games he compiled a 243-142 record with all but five wins coming as a Giant. In 457 starts he completed an amazing 244 games, and he racked up six 20-win seasons. And these stats are just the tip of the iceberg.

The statue dedication was attended by the other four living Giants Hall of Famers: Willie Mays, Willie McCovey, Orlando Cepeda and Gaylord Perry. Barry Bonds and many other Giants players were there as well. Even the president of the Dominican Republic, Leonel Fernandez, came for the statue dedication.

It was a wonderful day and very deserved for the "Dominican Dandy". As he ended his speech he said, "And last, but never least, I'd wish to extend my heartfelt thanks to the Giants fans for all their love and support throughout my career. As the songwriter once said, 'I Left My Heart in San Francisco'."

As for the 20,000 fans on August 16, 2015, who got a piece of history with the Marichal statue replicas …

They witnessed another legend-in-the-making.

Madison Bumgarner channeled his inner-Marichal and hurled a three-hit shutout, fanned 14 Nationals, and helped himself out by belting a homer.

The only other pitcher in Giants history to throw a shutout while striking out ten-plus batters *and* hitting a home run …

Juan Marichal.

…

In the sixth inning, it's all about "The Hurlers" … guys who can paint the corners and throw gas. Guys who aren't afraid to come high and tight and knock you off the plate. How much do you really know about these pitching legends?

TOP OF THE SIXTH

Q101: Nolan Ryan had a major-league record 15 seasons with 200-plus strikeouts. From 1958-2017, who had a Giants franchise record six seasons with 200-plus strikeouts?
   a) Juan Marichal
   b) Tim Lincecum
   c) Gaylord Perry
   d) Madison Bumgarner

Q102: In 1970, the Giants gave up 16 earned runs in a game vs. the San Diego Padres ... and won. It's the most earned runs given up in a win in San Francisco Giants history. As for individual pitchers, since the Giants moved west there has only been one pitcher in all of baseball to give up 10 earned runs and still record a win. And he did it for the Giants. Who got a win despite giving up 10 earned runs in six-plus innings vs. Milwaukee in May 2000?
   a) Livan Hernandez
   b) Russ Ortiz
   c) Mark Gardner
   d) Kirk Rueter

Q103: Christy Mathewson pitched an unusual complete game shutout vs. Cincinnati in 1914 ... in that game, Mathewson had zero walks and zero strikeouts. It was the first such game in franchise history, and it's been replicated only once since then. Who pitched a complete game four-hit shutout with no walks and no strikeouts for the 1976 Giants?
   a) Jim Barr
   b) John Montefusco
   c) Ed Halicki
   d) John D'Acquisto

Q104: Hank Aaron hit 67 home runs against San Francisco Giants pitching. That's the most allowed to any one player in team history. The guy second on that list hit 58 home runs—but he also has the distinction of striking out vs. Giants pitching more often than any player in history: 201 times. Which slugger was literally all-or-nothing vs. Giants pitching?

a) Willie Stargell
b) Matt Kemp
c) Tony Perez
d) Dale Murphy

Q105: Fans always love home wins, but they especially love home wins that end in strikeouts or walk-offs. Both are cool, both make us happy—and one pitcher sent fans home happy more than any other in team history. He ended the game with a strikeout 119 times. Maybe a save, maybe not—just saying he struck out a guy to end the game. Who is this pitcher?
   a) Robb Nen
   b) Rod Beck
   c) Brian Wilson
   d) Juan Marichal

Q106: In 1966, Juan Marichal pitched 307 1/3 innings and struck out 222 batters. Incredibly, he only gave up 36 walks. Among starters with at least 200 innings, his 6.17 strikeouts-to-walk ratio set a franchise record that lasted more than five decades. Who finally surpassed Marichal in the record book when he pitched 207 2/3 innings with 205 strikeouts and just 32 walks for a 6.41 strikeouts-to-walk ratio?
   a) Johnny Cueto
   b) Matt Cain
   c) Madison Bumgarner
   d) Jeff Samardzija

Q107: This pitcher is in a club with just one member … from 1958-2017, who is the only Giants pitcher to record 200 strikeouts while pitching fewer than 200 innings?
   a) Tim Lincecum
   b) Matt Cain
   c) Jonathan Sanchez
   d) Tim Hudson

Q108: Only one pitcher in franchise history has recorded a save in 10 consecutive appearances … and incredibly, he had four such streaks for the San Francisco Giants. Who is this stalwart closer?
   a) Rod Beck

b) Brian Wilson
c) Robb Nen
d) Tim Worrell

Q109: Here's an astounding number for you: 32. The Giants won an incredible 32 consecutive games in which Rod Beck appeared in 1993. That number is a franchise record … and it's actually been done twice. Who is the only other pitcher for which the Giants have won in 32 consecutive appearances?
   a) Sergio Romo
   b) Jeremy Affeldt
   c) Felix Rodriguez
   d) Robb Nen

Q110: This starting pitcher won nine games for the San Francisco Giants *before* his 20th birthday. He's the only teenager to start and win a game for the Giants since the club moved west in 1958. Who is this pitcher?
   a) Mike McCormick
   b) Pete Falcone
   c) Scott Garrelts
   d) Mark Grant

TOP OF THE SIXTH—ANSWER KEY

101: a. Juan Marichal.

102: b. Russ Ortiz.

103: a. Jim Barr.

104: d. Dale Murphy.

105: a. Robb Nen.

106: d. Jeff Samardzija.

107: c. Jonathan Sanchez.

108: a. Rod Beck.

109: d. Robb Nen.

110: a. Mike McCormick.

BOTTOM OF THE SIXTH

Q111: This pitcher won a franchise record 14 games on the road at Dodger Stadium—including five shutouts. Who ruined so many games for Dodgers fans?
   a) Gaylord Perry
   b) Barry Zito
   c) Juan Marichal
   d) Ed Halicki

Q112: In 1905, the New York Giants had five pitchers with 15 or more victories: Red Ames, Christy Mathewson, Joe McGinnity, Dummy Taylor, and Hooks Wiltse. No other team in franchise history has ever achieved this feat. The most 15-game winners in a season for the San Francisco Giants is four in 1962: Juan Marichal, Billy O'Dell, Billy Pierce, and Jack Sanford. Who led the Giants with 24 wins and placed second in Cy Young balloting in 1962?
   a) Juan Marichal
   b) Billy O'Dell
   c) Billy Pierce
   d) Jack Sanford

Q113: From 1958-2017, only one Giants pitcher had more than five games with 10 strikeouts and no walks. Who did this an astounding 12 times?
   a) Madison Bumgarner
   b) Tim Lincecum
   c) Juan Marichal
   d) Gaylord Perry

Q114: In 1898, lefty Cy Seymour had 239 strikeouts for the New York Giants. That number was a franchise record for lefties for a very long time. Which lefty finally surpassed it with 251 Ks in a season?
   a) Mike McCormick
   b) Carl Hubbell
   c) Madison Bumgarner
   d) Vida Blue

Q115: Through 2017, there have been only 23 perfect games in major-league history. Who pitched one for the Giants?
a) Christy Mathewson
b) Juan Marichal
c) Tim Lincecum
d) Matt Cain

Q116: Hall of Fame legend Sandy Koufax and Tim Lincecum are the only pitchers in major-league history with multiple no-hitters, multiple Cy Young Awards, multiple All-Star selections, and multiple World Series titles. Not bad, right? Lincecum is also the only pitcher in history to no-hit the same team in consecutive seasons. Against which team did he pitch no-hitters in 2013 and 2014?
a) Los Angeles Dodgers
b) San Diego Padres
c) Arizona Diamondbacks
d) Colorado Rockies

Q117: Christy Mathewson led the NL in ERA five times. No San Francisco Giants pitcher has ever led the league in ERA more than once. Through 2017, who is the most recent Giant to win an ERA title?
a) Juan Marichal
b) Madison Bumgarner
c) Jason Schmidt
d) Bill Swift

Q118: Juan Marichal made his major-league debut on July 19, 1960. How did he do? You be the judge: nine innings, one hit, 12 strikeouts, one walk, no runs. I think he did okay. Only one other player has ever pitched a complete game shutout in his major-league debut with the San Francisco Giants. Which hurler achieved this amazing feat?
a) Noah Lowry
b) Mike Remlinger
c) John Montefusco
d) Steve Stone

Q119: And a follow-up to that last question … who is the only player in San Francisco Giants history to pitch two complete game shutouts within

his first 10 major-league starts?
- a) Noah Lowry
- b) Mike Remlinger
- c) John Montefusco
- d) Steve Stone

Q120: This pitcher had a major-league debut unlike any other player in the history of the game. Not an exaggeration. He is literally the only pitcher in baseball history to debut in relief, pitch nine innings, and earn the victory. Ron Bryant started and faced six batters vs. the Los Angeles Dodgers. He didn't get an out. Cue the rookie, for his big-league debut. Nine innings, six hits, one run, seven strikeouts … for the win. One more crazy fact. *He also hit a home run.* Whose debut was truly historic?
- a) Noah Lowry
- b) Mike Remlinger
- c) John Montefusco
- d) Steve Stone

BOTTOM OF THE SIXTH—ANSWER KEY

111: c. Juan Marichal.

112: d. Jack Sanford.

113: a. Madison Bumgarner.

114: c. Madison Bumgarner.

115: d. Matt Cain.

116: b. San Diego Padres.

117: c. Jason Schmidt.

118: b. Mike Remlinger.

119: c. John Montefusco.

120: c. John Montefusco.

Cruz waiting on Wilson. And the right hander for the Giants throws. Swing and a miss! And that's it! The Giants—for the first time in 52 years—the Giants are world champions!

Duane Kuiper

7

THE term "walk-off" has become part of baseball's vernacular. It is that moment when all is on the line and the home team comes through. It's a bleeder down the right field line, a monstrous home run, an actual walk, a sacrifice fly … it's anything that ends the game in dramatic fashion and gives the home team the win.

When it comes to World Series victories no team has been more prominent in recent years than the San Francisco Giants with three titles since 2010, but oddly enough, the Giants have never even had the opportunity for a walk-off win since every series has been clinched on the road.

That leads us to final outs.

It might not be as dramatic as walk-offs, but when you've been holding your breath for the last half-inning, hoping that your team can seal the deal, there isn't much that's sweeter than the final out.

For the Giants, the first final out came on November 1, 2010. The club was up three-games to one and playing in Arlington against the Rangers. Edgar Renteria had blasted a three-run shot in the seventh and now in the bottom of the ninth Brian Wilson was tasked with getting out the heart of the Rangers lineup to preserve the win and finally bring a World Series home to San Francisco.

Wilson struck out Josh Hamilton looking, got Vladimir Guerrero to ground out, and then faced Nelson Cruz (who homered in his previous at bat). Cruz was down in the count but worked it full.

Wilson cut loose.

Cruz swung … strike three!

The Giants celebrated on the Rangers' field.

Fast-forward two years. Giants pitching had dominated the Tigers in route to a three-game lead. Now it was the bottom of the tenth of Game 4. The Giants had just taken a 4-3 lead in the top half, and now Sergio Romero toed the rubber. He promptly struck out Austin Jackson and Don Kelly, but the dangerous Miguel Cabrera was at the plate. With the count 2-2, Romero fired and Cabrera watched it go by, strike three! In a three-season span the Giants had claimed two titles!

Fast-forward two more years.

It's October 29, 2014. Game 7. As intense as it gets. Two outs and Alex Gordon stands just 90 feet away from tying it up. The count is 2-2, and Madison Bumgarner delivers to Salvador Perez. He swings and pops it up in foul territory. Third baseman Pablo Sandoval makes the play and in a five-season span the Giants clinched the title three times, all on the road.

Would Giants fans have loved a walk-off?

You bet.

Are they complaining about these final outs?

Not on your life.

...

In the seventh inning we turn our attention to "Fantastic Feats" … the wild, crazy, seemingly unbelievable, and yet true achievements from your all-time favorite Giants. You ready for this?

TOP OF THE SEVENTH

Q121: Andrew McCutchen had six hits in a 7-5 victory over the Los Angeles Dodgers in April 2018. The newly acquired outfielder was just the fourth member of the San Francisco Giants to record six or more hits in one game. McCutchen, however, was one hit shy of the franchise record. Who had seven hits in a game vs. the Miami Marlins?
  a) Hunter Pence
  b) Denard Span
  c) Brandon Belt
  d) Brandon Crawford

Q122: This all-time great tied a major-league record when he had nine hits during a doubleheader vs. the Dodgers. He was 9-for-10 with a home run and five RBIs on the day. Who accomplished this extraordinary feat?
  a) Orlando Cepeda
  b) Mel Ott
  c) Willie Mays
  d) Bill Terry

Q123: In 1928, Mel Ott became a permanent fixture in the Giants outfield. And how did he respond? Well, he led the club in home runs … and then he repeated that feat, again, and again, and again, for every single full-season that he spent with the club. What is the unbelievable number of consecutive seasons in which Mel Ott led the Giants in home runs?
  a) 15
  b) 16
  c) 17
  d) 18

Q124: In one of the most extraordinary performances in major-league history, this Giants pitcher had a complete game, 18-inning shutout vs. St. Louis. You read it right: *18 innings*. At one point in the contest he had 12 consecutive perfect innings. All total he faced 59 batters, gave up six hits, no walks, and had 12 strikeouts in the 1-0 victory. Whose arm gave the Giants one of the best pitched games in major-league history?
  a) Christy Mathewson

b) Juan Marichal
c) Carl Hubbell
d) Gaylord Perry

Q125: Bob Gibson was one of the most intimidating pitchers in baseball for more than a decade in the 1960s and 1970s. But one member of the San Francisco Giants went head-to-head with Gibson and came out on top in historic fashion: a 1-0 victory and a no-hitter vs. a powerful St. Louis Cardinals lineup. Who no-hit the Cards in a showdown with Bob Gibson?
   a) Gaylord Perry
   b) Juan Marichal
   c) Mike McCormick
   d) Ray Sadecki

Q126: In the first at-bat of his major-league career, this rookie hit a long home run against future Hall of Fame legend Nolan Ryan. A week later he had three hits and a home run in his first-ever game at Candlestick Park. Who began his career with such spectacular feats?
   a) Will Clark
   b) Robby Thompson
   c) Matt Williams
   d) Jack Clark

Q127: Only three players have scored five runs in a game for the San Francisco Giants. For good measure, one of them did it in a three-homer game. Who had three home runs *and* a franchise record five runs in a single-game?
   a) Willie Mays
   b) Matt Williams
   c) J.T. Snow
   d) Barry Bonds

Q128: And a follow-up to that last question … who is the only player in San Francisco Giants history to score a record five runs in a game *twice* in the same season?
   a) Willie Mays
   b) Matt Williams
   c) J.T. Snow

d) Barry Bonds

Q129: Barry Bonds homered in six consecutive games in April 2001 … and then he homered in six consecutive games, again, just one month later. Twice in one season. Just, extraordinary. He also holds the franchise record with home runs in seven consecutive games in 2004. Willie Mays had a streak of six consecutive games with a home run in 1965. The longest non-Bonds/Mays streak in team history is five. Who are the only players not named Bonds or Mays to homer in five consecutive games for the San Francisco Giants?
   a) Brandon Belt/Hunter Pence
   b) Robby Thompson/Jack Clark
   c) Jeff Kent/Rich Aurilia
   d) Kevin Mitchell/Will Clark

Q130: In San Francisco Giants history, one player scored at least one run in a team record 14 consecutive games. Who achieved this fantastic feat?
   a) Dan Gladden
   b) Bobby Bonds
   c) Andres Torres
   d) Willie Mays

TOP OF THE SEVENTH—ANSWER KEY

121: d. Brandon Crawford.

122: d. Bill Terry.

123: d. 18.

124: c. Carl Hubbell.

125: a. Gaylord Perry.

126: a. Will Clark.

127: c. J.T. Snow.

128: a. Willie Mays.

129: b. Robby Thompson/Jack Clark.

130: d. Willie Mays.

BOTTOM OF THE SEVENTH

Q131: This pitcher set a major-league record with 20 consecutive wins over two seasons. He said afterward, "When I lose, they'll have to knock me out of there. I'm not going to let this streak worry me and walk them around the bases." He ran his record streak to 24 consecutive wins before the Dodgers finally brought it to an end. Who is this extraordinary pitcher?
 a) Christy Mathewson
 b) Juan Marichal
 c) Carl Hubbell
 d) Gaylord Perry

Q132: In the midst of a six-game road trip in late September 2010, with a narrow half-game lead in the division and a postseason berth hanging in the balance, this player led an historic offensive outburst to give the Giants a much-needed win against the Chicago Cubs. He had two home runs and six RBIs ... *in one inning*. Who paced the Giants to a 13-0 victory to stay atop the division?
 a) Juan Uribe
 b) Buster Posey
 c) Pablo Sandoval
 d) Aaron Rowand

Q133: Hall of Famer Hack Wilson was the first player in franchise history with two homers in one inning. He did it on July 1, 1925, in the second game of a doubleheader vs. the Phillies. Who is the only player in franchise history with two homers in one inning ... *twice*?
 a) Hack Wilson
 b) Pablo Sandoval
 c) Willie Mays
 d) Willie McCovey

Q134: This Hall of Fame pitcher hit a home run in his first major-league at-bat ... and then never hit another one for the rest of his career. Who did this for the Giants?
 a) Hoyt Wilhelm
 b) Carl Hubbell

c) Juan Marichal
d) Gaylord Perry

Q135: A no-hitter is a rare and spectacular feat. A no-hitter by a *rookie* is something else entirely. It's happened just three times in more than 135 years of franchise history. The first was Christy Mathewson in 1901. The second was Jeff Tesreau in 1912. And the third? He did it for the San Francisco Giants. Who pitched a no-hitter during his rookie campaign?
 a) Tim Lincecum
 b) Jonathan Sanchez
 c) Chris Heston
 d) John Montefusco

Q136: This player had a month to remember: he batted .417 with a 21-game hitting streak, 24 RBIs, and 43 hits … *as a rookie*. It's the longest rookie hitting streak in San Francisco Giants history. Who achieved this extraordinary feat?
 a) Willie McCovey
 b) Jack Clark
 c) Buster Posey
 d) Garry Maddox

Q137: The San Francisco Giants record for consecutive multi-hit games is seven. Through 2017, eight different players have achieved this feat—most recently Marco Scutaro in 2013—and one player had three such streaks. Who had three streaks of seven consecutive games with multiple hits?
 a) Jeff Kent
 b) Orlando Cepeda
 c) Stan Javier
 d) Willie Mays

Q138: The San Francisco Giants record for consecutive games with an extra-base hit is nine. Through 2017, it's been done only three times. Orlando Cepeda was the first back in 1961. Willie Mays was the second in 1963. Who was the most recent player with an extra-base hit in nine consecutive games?
 a) Barry Bonds
 b) Pablo Sandoval

c) Brandon Belt
d) J.T. Snow

Q139: Who is the only pitcher in San Francisco Giants history to toss four consecutive complete game shutouts? In 36 innings, he gave up just 15 hits and three walks while recording 20 strikeouts.
   a) Livan Hernandez
   b) Juan Marichal
   c) Vida Blue
   d) Gaylord Perry

Q140: This record is untouchable the way baseball is played nowadays ... who pitched a San Francisco Giants record 20 consecutive complete games? He was 17-3 in that stretch with five shutouts.
   a) Mike McCormick
   b) Juan Marichal
   c) Vida Blue
   d) Gaylord Perry

BOTTOM OF THE SEVENTH—ANSWER KEY

131: c. Carl Hubbell.

132: a. Juan Uribe.

133: d. Willie McCovey.

134: a. Hoyt Wilhelm.

135: c. Chris Heston.

136: c. Buster Posey.

137: d. Willie Mays.

138: b. Pablo Sandoval.

139: d. Gaylord Perry.

140: b. Juan Marichal.

At the end of the game, it was the greatest feeling in the world. It was the greatest high that I have ever experienced in my life. The adrenalin that I felt in the ninth inning was incredible. I didn't care who came up to bat in the ninth inning, because the adrenalin that was rushing through my body would have allowed me to get Willie Mays, Joe DiMaggio, Babe Ruth, Mickey Mantle, Lou Gehrig and anybody else out in that ninth inning.

John Montefusco

8

ONE of the great things about going to the ballpark is that something magical could happen on any given night. Is your favorite player Hunter Pence? Maybe he'll hit a cycle for you. Love Brandon Crawford? He could belt three dingers. Think Brandon Belt has a sweet swing? He could rip four or five hits, easy.

Oh, you like hurlers?

Let's fire up a no-hitter. Lincecum, anyone?

That's the beauty of this game. You just never know.

And when it comes to magical moments, few things in professional sports can top a no-hitter. The first for the San Francisco Giants was delivered at Candlestick Park by the high-kicking Juan Marichal on June 15, 1963. Marichal sat down five Houston Colt .45 batters and walked two on his way into the record books.

Want more no-no's?

Gaylord Perry, Ed Halicki, and John Montefusco all hurled no-no's over the next 13 years.

Hey, it can't be magical if it happens *every* night. It's the anticipation and knowing that it *could* happen tonight that makes us dream. And after Montefusco it was like crickets at the ballpark when it came to Giants no-hitters. For the rest of the '70s, '80s, and '90s.

Then came Jonathan Sanchez.

He faced just one over the minimum and ended a 33-year no-no drought. Matt Cain was perfect just three years later. A year later Tim Lincecum no-hit the Padres. He had so much fun doing it, that he no-hit the Padres a second time the following year.

The most magical no-hitter was probably on June 9, 2015.

Chris Heston shut down the New York Mets by striking out 11 in route to a 5-0 victory. He did plunk three batters, but other than that he was superlative.

He was also a rookie.

His aunt, Dawn Chapman, drove to New York from Cleveland and said, "All the way out there I was driving and saying, 'Perfect game. Perfect game. Perfect game.' And my friend said, 'Just a good game.' I said, 'No, no, we strive for perfection.' Very close!"

Heston said, "Just to even have the opportunity to be out there, I'm really blessed. And it was a lot of fun!"

Now Heston's name is etched in the Giants record book with the likes of Marichal, Perry, Halicki, Montefusco, Sanchez, Cain, and Lincecum.

Fun?

Oh yeah, and magical.

...

In the eighth inning our focus shifts to "Award Winners" ... guys who earned hardware thanks to extraordinary talent, hard work, and the will to persevere. It's getting late in the game ... think you have the knowledge to close this thing out with a W?

TOP OF THE EIGHTH

Q141: This pitcher was the first-ever unanimous winner of the National League Most Valuable Player Award when he led the league with 26 wins and a 2.31 ERA. Not a big surprise, but the Giants also won the pennant that same year. Who is this award-winning pitcher?
 a) Christy Mathewson
 b) Juan Marichal
 c) Carl Hubbell
 d) Gaylord Perry

Q142: In his major-league debut, this slugger was 4-for-4 with two triples against Philadelphia Phillies pitcher Robin Roberts. It was a sign of things to come, as he would go on to win Rookie of the Year honors. Who began his career with a perfect day against a future Hall of Fame pitcher?
 a) Willie Mays
 b) Orlando Cepeda
 c) Bobby Bonds
 d) Willie McCovey

Q143: This pitcher won 15 games with four shutouts and 215 strikeouts during his rookie season. All three numbers are rookie records for San Francisco. For his efforts he won Rookie of the Year honors. Who is this outstanding talent?
 a) John D'Acquisto
 b) John Montefusco
 c) Tim Lincecum
 d) Matt Cain

Q144: There are multiple Gold Glove-winning shortstops in Giants history. The same is true for second base. But shortstop and second base in the same season? It's happened once. Who were the first middle infielders to win Gold Glove Awards in the same season for the Giants?
 a) Omar Vizquel/Ray Durham
 b) Brandon Crawford/Joe Panik
 c) Royce Clayton/Robby Thompson
 d) Rich Aurilia/Jeff Kent

Q145: In 1997, Barry Bonds won a Silver Slugger Award and a Gold Glove. It took nearly 20 years before another Giants player accomplished this feat. Who won both a Silver Slugger and a Gold Glove in 2015?
   a) Buster Posey
   b) Madison Bumgarner
   c) Brandon Crawford
   d) Joe Panik

Q146: In 1980, Jack Clark was the first-ever winner of the Willie Mac Award. The award is named for Willie McCovey, obviously, and is given annually to the most inspirational player on the team as voted by players, coaches, and, in recent years, fans. Who is the only rookie to ever be given this prestigious award?
   a) Matt Cain
   b) Buster Posey
   c) Matt Duffy
   d) Brandon Crawford

Q147: Buster Posey won the NL batting title in 2012 with the third highest average by a NL catcher since the Giants moved west in 1958. Posey was also the National League MVP in 2012. He joined Willie Mays and Barry Bonds as Giants who won a batting title and MVP in the same season. What was Posey's league-best average?
   a) .306
   b) .316
   c) .326
   d) .336

Q148: This player was a trade deadline acquisition in 2012. All he did was hit .362 in 61 games down the stretch. And in October? He hit .500 in the NLCS and won series MVP honors as the Giants eliminated the Cardinals en route to a world championship. Who is this award-winner?
   a) Hunter Pence
   b) Marco Scutaro
   c) Ryan Theriot
   d) Angel Pagan

Q149: Teammates Jeff Kent and Barry Bonds finished one-two in MVP

balloting in 2000. It was only the sixth time during baseball's divisional era that teammates placed first and second in the MVP race—but it was the second time that teammates did it for the Giants. Which other duo accomplished this rare feat?
   a) Willie Mays/Willie McCovey
   b) Orlando Cepeda/Bobby Bonds
   c) Barry Bonds/Matt Williams
   d) Kevin Mitchell/Will Clark

Q150: Who won the Manager of the Year Award after he led the club to a San Francisco-era best 103 wins during his first-ever season as a big-league manager?
   a) Alvin Dark
   b) Frank Robinson
   c) Dusty Baker
   d) Bruce Bochy

TOP OF THE EIGHTH—ANSWER KEY

141: c. Carl Hubbell.

142: d. Willie McCovey.

143: b. John Montefusco.

144: b. Brandon Crawford/Joe Panik (2016).

145: c. Brandon Crawford.

146: c. Matt Duffy.

147: d. .336.

148: b. Marco Scutaro.

149: c. Kevin Mitchell/Will Clark (1989).

150: c. Dusty Baker.

BOTTOM OF THE EIGHTH

Q151: Who is the only three-time Manager of the Year recipient in franchise history?
   a) Bruce Bochy
   b) Dusty Baker
   c) Alvin Dark
   d) Leo Durocher

Q152: The Hank Aaron Award was first given in 1999 by Major League Baseball to recognize the top hitter in each league. Barry Bonds won the award three times. Through 2017, who is the only other Giant to receive this prestigious award?
   a) Buster Posey
   b) Jeff Kent
   c) Pablo Sandoval
   d) Rich Aurilia

Q153: Willie Mays won 1954 MVP honors for the New York Giants, and then 11 years later he won 1965 MVP honors for the San Francisco Giants. Not bad. Willie McCovey was the second player to win MVP honors in San Francisco. In what year did McCovey lead the league with 45 home runs and 126 RBIs on his way to winning MVP honors?
   a) 1967
   b) 1968
   c) 1969
   d) 1970

Q154: Barry Bonds won MVP honors more than any player in history. How many times was he MVP in San Francisco?
   a) 3
   b) 4
   c) 5
   d) 6

Q155: Barry Bonds won his first MVP in 1993. The Giants had Mays and McCovey in the 1960s, Bonds in the 1990s, and ... who was the only player

to win MVP honors for the Giants in the 1970s or 1980s?
a) Bobby Bonds
b) Jack Clark
c) Kevin Mitchell
d) Will Clark

Q156: You need to go all the way back to 1912 for this one … who won the first MVP Award of the modern era for the Giants franchise?
a) Larry Doyle
b) Christy Mathewson
c) Fred Merkle
d) Rube Marquard

Q157: Prior to Buster Posey in 2010, who was the last position player to win Rookie of the Year for the Giants?
a) Larry Herndon
b) Gary Matthews
c) Dave Rader
d) Willie McCovey

Q158: The Comeback Player of the Year Award is significant because it recognizes perseverance through adversity. Buster Posey won this award in 2012 after a devastating injury a year earlier could easily have ended his career. Who was the first player in franchise history to be given this honor?
a) Joe Morgan
b) Willie McCovey
c) Mike McCormick
d) Orlando Cepeda

Q159: The Silver Slugger Award has been given annually since 1980. It recognizes the best offensive player at each position in both leagues. Who was the first Giant to win this prestigious award?
a) Don Robinson
b) Kevin Mitchell
c) Will Clark
d) Joe Morgan

Q160: Willie Mays won 12 Gold Glove Awards for the Giants. His defensive prowess is as legendary as his ability to hit. Truly, he is the greatest player ever. Mays dominated this award—he won it every year from 1957-68. In that span, there was one season in which the Giants had two award-winning outfielders. Who was the first Giants outfielder—other than Willie Mays—to win a Gold Glove?

a) Willie Kirkland
b) Jackie Brandt
c) Felipe Alou
d) Leon Wagner

BOTTOM OF THE EIGHTH—ANSWER KEY

151: b. Dusty Baker.

152: a. Buster Posey.

153: c. 1969.

154: c. 5.

155: c. Kevin Mitchell (1989).

156: a. Larry Doyle.

157: b. Gary Matthews (1973).

158: c. Mike McCormick (1967).

159: d. Joe Morgan (1982).

160: b. Jackie Brandt (1959).

These pretzels are making me thirsty.

Hunter Pence/*Seinfeld*

9

Sometimes a baseball team has a player that everyone latches onto. The fans connect with that player in a way that is hard to explain. In recent years, that player for the Giants has been the herky-jerky right fielder, Hunter Pence.

There is a reason for his unique style of play. It was recently discovered that Pence had Scheuermann's Disease, a spinal disorder that affects vertebrae and reduces flexibility. It hasn't affected his play in the least. He's a three-time All-Star and has been steady for the Giants since coming to the club in 2012.

Pence is no doubt a great baseball player, but there's something more that makes him a fan-favorite.

Maybe it's his "Yes! Yes! Yes!" chant that motivates the crowd heading into the postseason? Or because he rolls to work on his scooter? Then again, it could be that he was the brunt of the hilarious campaign where opposing teams' fans mocked him with weirdly specific signs, like, "Hunter Pence can't parallel park."

And he loved it.

He even made a funny video that confirmed many of the goofy insults were in fact true.

In reality, it's probably a combination of all of the above. Giants fans love Pence because he is a great baseball player who is easy to connect with and seems like he could be one of the guys hanging out at the barbeque cheering the team on to another World Series victory.

He's one of many reasons to be a San Francisco Giants fan and here's to hoping he leads many more "Yes! Yes! Yes!" chants.

...

Closer time is all about "The Teams" … if your trivia skills are Robb Nen-esque, then the ninth inning won't be a problem. The game is on the line. Are you nervous?

TOP OF THE NINTH

Q161: The New York Giants were the first team in major-league history to feature an all African American outfield when Monte Irvin, Hank Thompson and Willie Mays started Game 1 of the World Series together vs. an all-white New York Yankees. What year did the Giants make history vs. the Yankees?
    a) 1951
    b) 1952
    c) 1953
    d) 1954

Q162: Through 2017, the longest home winning streak at AT&T Park is 11 games. Which division champion team set this mark?
    a) 2000
    b) 2003
    c) 2010
    d) 2012

Q163: From September 2002 through April 2003, the Giants won 11 consecutive road games. That's the best road streak for the Giants since moving west. However, it spanned two seasons. The best in-season road winning streak is nine games. Which team set this mark?
    a) 1966
    b) 1976
    c) 1986
    d) 1996

Q164: From 1958-2017, a total of 60 seasons, the San Francisco Giants have played .500 or better against the Dodgers 33 times. The Giants have won 10 or more games vs. the Dodgers in 21 of 60 seasons out west. The most season wins vs. the Dodgers in that span is 16. Which team had a very satisfying 16-6 record against its most-hated rival?
    a) 1958
    b) 1988
    c) 2010
    d) 2012

Q165: The 1962 Giants won a franchise record 103 games but lost to the Yankees in the World Series. Which team actually missed the postseason despite a record-tying 103 regular season wins?
   a) 1987
   b) 1993
   c) 1995
   d) 1997

Q166: This Giants team finished second despite setting two franchise records: 19 shutouts and a 2.71 team ERA. Which team could have used a little more offense to backup its pitching staff?
   a) 1968
   b) 1974
   c) 1987
   d) 1991

Q167: From 1958-2017, the team record for home runs in a season is 235. You know this has to be a Barry Bonds-led team, right? Which team hit 235 bombs?
   a) 2001
   b) 2002
   c) 2003
   d) 2004

Q168: The San Francisco Giants have hit six or more home runs in a game 11 times. Not a surprise, but they've won all 11 of those games. The record for most team home runs in a game is eight. Which team hit eight bombs in a 14-4 drubbing of Milwaukee?
   a) 2002
   b) 1961
   c) 2001
   d) 1963

Q169: The Giants once played a 23-inning game vs. the Mets. It was on the road at Shea Stadium and, worse, it was also the backend of a doubleheader. The Giants prevailed 8-6 when pinch-hitter Del Crandall hit a two-out RBI double. Crandall was hitting for Gaylord Perry, who pitched an astonishing 10 scoreless innings out of the bullpen. Perry and five other pitchers

combined for a franchise record 22 strikeouts. Which team played this extraordinary game?
 a) 1962
 b) 1964
 c) 1966
 d) 1968

Q170: The Giants had nine seasons from 1958-2017 in which their starting pitchers recorded 10 or more strikeouts in 10 or more games. Got that? The team record is 14 such games in one season. Which teams share this record?
 a) 1964/1975
 b) 2016/2017
 c) 2008/2010
 d) 1968/2011

TOP OF THE NINTH—ANSWER KEY

161: a. 1951.

162: b. 2003.

163: a. 1966.

164: a. 1958.

165: b. 1993.

166: a. 1968.

167: a. 2001.

168: b. 1961.

169: b. 1964.

170: c. 2008/2010.

BOTTOM OF THE NINTH

Q171: This team won more extra-inning games than any other in San Francisco Giants history: 14. Jim Ray Hart, Orlando Cepeda and Willie Mays were the stars on offense. Juan Marichal anchored the pitching staff. Which team was so clutch while giving fans free baseball?
   a) 1958
   b) 1961
   c) 1964
   d) 1967

Q172: This team set a San Francisco record with 15 walk-off wins in one season. David Green led the way with four walk-off hits. One left the yard. All total eight different batters got in on the heroics, and the Giants walked-off against eight different opponents. Ready for the crazy part? The Giants won just 38 home games all season … 15 out of 38 were walk-offs. The club won just 62 games total … nearly one-quarter of the Giants wins were walk-offs. Truly crazy. Which team was the most exciting last-place club in franchise history?
   a) 1979
   b) 1982
   c) 1985
   d) 1988

Q173: From 2000-09, the Giants hit 1,660 home runs for the most powerful decade in franchise history. However, that total was actually only tenth best among National League teams. In which decade—and for the only time in franchise history—did the Giants hit more home runs than any other NL team?
   a) 1960s
   b) 1970s
   c) 1980s
   d) 1990s

Q174: A lot of powerful hitters suited it up for the Giants. Many had multiple 20-home run seasons. But only twice in franchise history has the club boasted five players each with 20-plus home runs in the same season.

Some hints: Felipe Alou was one of the five the first time, and J.T. Snow was one of the five the second time. In which seasons did the Giants boast five players each with 20-plus home runs?
   a) 1958/2004
   b) 1963/1999
   c) 1965/2001
   d) 1961/2002

Q175: The longest team home run streak in San Francisco Giants history is 16 games. It's been done twice, and in consecutive seasons. In which seasons did the Giants hit at least one home run in 16 consecutive games?
   a) 2001/2002
   b) 2010/2011
   c) 1962/1963
   d) 1958/1959

Q176: From September 2002 through April 2003, the Giants scored at least five runs in nine consecutive games. That tied the longest streak in franchise history—however, the other nine-game streak was in a single-season. In which season did the Giants score five or more runs in a franchise best nine consecutive games?
   a) 1993
   b) 2000
   c) 2007
   d) 2010

Q177: The most home wins in Candlestick Park history is 61. Which team set this record?
   a) 1962
   b) 1971
   c) 1987
   d) 1989

Q178: Through 2017, the Giants have scored 10 or more runs at Dodger Stadium 16 times—including one game in which the Giants scored 19 times. In which disappointing season did the Giants take out their frustration by humiliating LA 19-3 at Dodger Stadium in late September?
   a) 2011

b) 2013
c) 2015
d) 2017

Q179: In one season the Giants had four starters rank among the top 11 league leaders in ERA. Plus, three starters and the Giants closer were All-Stars ... and the staff's 3.20 ERA was second-best in the league. The problem was injuries on offense. The Giants had more players on the disabled list than any team in baseball and scored a league worst 570 runs. As a result the Giants missed the postseason despite being so dominant on the mound. In which season could the Giants have used another bat?
   a) 2007
   b) 2009
   c) 2011
   d) 2013

Q180: In which season did the Giants sell out every home game at AT&T Park and set an attendance record with 3,387,303 joyous fans?
   a) 2011
   b) 2013
   c) 2015
   d) 2017

BOTTOM OF THE NINTH—ANSWER KEY

171: c. 1964.

172: c. 1985.

173: a. 1960s.

174: b. 1963/1999.

175: c. 1962/1963.

176: a. 1993.

177: a. 1962.

178: b. 2013.

179: c. 2011.

180: a. 2011.

I can't tell you about moments because I wasn't into that. I just played every day and enjoyed what I was doing. When I made a great catch it was just routine. I didn't worry about it. Winning was important. Winning.

Willie Mays

10

HE'D been called baseball's best dressed pinch-hitter by Fred Lieb because he reportedly owned over one hundred suits, but on April 30, 1944, Phil "Mickey" Weintraub was simply baseball's best hitter. On that day, Weintraub and the Giants took on the hated Dodgers and destroyed them, 26-8. Weintraub led the way with two doubles, a triple and a home run, while knocking in a ridiculous 11 runs!

The RBI total is still a Giants record to this day.

Fast-forward exactly 17 years from the day when Weintraub was baseball's best hitter and you'll find someone much more prolific at the plate. Willie Mays had already been an All-Star for numerous seasons and had claimed the MVP. He was already regarded as one of the best hitters in baseball, but then on April 30, 1961, he had a truly special game.

The Giants were at Milwaukee, and Mays blasted a home run in the first. The Braves came back with three in the bottom of the first thanks to a three-run shot by Hank Aaron, but there was no way Mays would let that lead hold.

In the top of the third he belted his second dinger, this one a two-run shot. And he wasn't finished, not by a long shot. In the top of the sixth he hit his third home run of the game, a three-run shot over the left field wall.

In the bottom of the sixth Hank Aaron hit another homer in an effort to keep pace, but Willie came to bat again in the top of the eighth and blasted another two-run shot over the left-center field wall. It was his fourth homer of the game and he'd knocked in eight runs!

Amazingly, the Giants actually hit eight homers on the day. Jose Pagan added two and Felipe Alou and Orlando Cepeda each hit one. It was an amazing night for Mays and the Giants.

So on April 30, 1944, Weintraub was the best hitter in baseball for the day. On April 30, 1961, Willie Mays proved that he was the best hitter in baseball, period.

Both nights are still etched in the Giants record book as no other player has racked up 11 RBIs or four dingers in a single game.

...

There is no clock in baseball. You have to get 27 outs, and then you can go home. That's why you never leave a game early. You just don't know what's going to happen next. But sometimes 27 outs aren't enough. It's "Extra Innings" time, and it could go all night. Tense. Exhilarating. And conventional wisdom is tossed. Everything is on the table, because all it takes to win is a single run. That's why here in extras we've got a bit of everything trivia-wise … will you send everyone home happy with a walk-off?

TOP OF THE TENTH

Q181: Only eight players ever hit 20 or more home runs in a single-season at Candlestick Park. Bobby Bonds and Barry Bonds both did it. As did Willie Mays and Willie McCovey. The record is 28. Who set a franchise season record with 28 home runs at The Stick?
   a) Matt Williams
   b) Kevin Mitchell
   c) Bobby Bonds
   d) Willie Mays

Q182: In 1973, Dave Rader had a franchise record streak of 20 consecutive games without a strikeout—and he had at least three plate appearances per game. In 2002, Barry Bonds tied Rader's record streak. Who set a new standard in 2015 when he had a streak of 21 games with no strikeouts and at least three plate appearances per game?
   a) Buster Posey
   b) Joe Panik
   c) Norichika Aoki
   d) Angel Pagan

Q183: You generally think of shortstops as being defensive leaders rather than guys who pace the offense. The guys who really thump the ball end up switching from short to third base more times than not. However, a few guys through the years have provided the Giants with stellar play at shortstop while swinging a big stick. Take this player, for example … who is the only shortstop in San Francisco Giants history to lead the team in RBIs?
   a) Rich Aurilia
   b) Brandon Crawford
   c) Royce Clayton
   d) Jose Pagan

Q184: It's a long season, and the wear and tear and grind of it all takes a physical toll on players. That's why games played records are so impressive. Who was the first player in San Francisco Giants history to play all 162 games in a single-season?

a) Darrell Evans
b) Jack Clark
c) Will Clark
d) Hunter Pence

Q185: The Giants had less than 24 hours to prepare for the Yankees after Bobby Thomson's heroics won the 1951 pennant. The World Series began the very next day. A letdown would have been understandable … but instead this player ignited the offense with a straight steal of home in the first inning, and the Giants took the opener 5-1. Who stole home in Game 1 of the 1951 World Series?
a) Willie Mays
b) Bobby Thomson
c) Monte Irvin
d) Eddie Stanky

Q186: This player made his major-league debut on September 11, 1985, and promptly hit safely in his first 13 games. No other player in franchise history has even come close to that number. Who achieved this remarkable feat?
a) Matt Nokes
b) Chris Brown
c) Tom O'Malley
d) Mike Woodard

Q187: The Giants had 26,400 hits all-time at Candlestick Park. Which Giant had more Candlestick hits than any other player in history?
a) Bobby Bonds
b) Will Clark
c) Willie Mays
d) Willie McCovey

Q188: And a follow-up to that last question … the Giants had 256 walk-off hits at Candlestick Park. Which Giant had the most walk-off hits in Candlestick Park history?
a) Jack Clark
b) Will Clark
c) Matt Williams

d) Jim Davenport

Q189: Who is the only pitcher in franchise history to save 100 games at Candlestick Park?
a) Greg Minton
b) Robb Nen
c) Steve Bedrosian
d) Rod Beck

Q190: It was team owner Horace Stoneham who moved the Giants from New York to San Francisco. Stoneham, when asked how it felt to be the guy taking baseball away from kids in New York, replied, "I feel bad about the kids, but I haven't seen many of their fathers lately." Attendance wasn't a problem at Seals Stadium when the club began play in 1958. The stadium was packed for the first-ever meeting of the San Francisco Giants and Los Angeles Dodgers. Who pitched a complete game shutout in that historic game?
a) Ruben Gomez
b) Johnny Antonelli
c) Mike McCormick
d) Stu Miller

TOP OF THE TENTH—ANSWER KEY

181: d. Willie Mays.

182: c. Norichika Aoki.

183: b. Brandon Crawford.

184: d. Hunter Pence (2013).

185: c. Monte Irvin.

186: d. Mike Woodard.

187: d. Willie McCovey.

188: a. Jack Clark.

189: d. Rod Beck.

190: a. Ruben Gomez.

BOTTOM OF THE TENTH

Q191: This player began the 2018 season by writing his name in the record books. He was the first player in major-league history to homer in back-to-back 1-0 ballgames. And he did it in the first two games of the season, against the defending league champion Dodgers, against two of the best pitchers on the planet: Clayton Kershaw and Kenley Jansen. Who began 2018 in such fine form?
    a) Brandon Belt
    b) Joe Panik
    c) Brandon Crawford
    d) Andrew McCutchen

Q192: Felipe Alou took over as manager of the Giants in 2003, and his club became just the second in franchise history—and only the tenth in major-league history—to go wire-to-wire on the season. The Giants won 100 games and led the Dodgers by 15 1/2 games at season's end. It was the Dodgers worst finish in relation to the Giants in nearly a century, which was just fine with Giants fans. It was also the first time in a very long time that the Giants made consecutive appearances in the postseason. Prior to 2002-03, when was the last time the Giants made back-to-back trips to the postseason?
    a) 1936-37
    b) 1951-52
    c) 1954-55
    d) 1988-89

Q193: The Giants bid to repeat as league champions in 2003 produced one of the most thrilling plays of the decade ... unfortunately, it went in favor of the Marlins. The Giants faced elimination in Game 4, and trailed by two runs in the top of the ninth. With two outs and the tying run on second, Jeffrey Hammonds lined a single to left ... only the runner was cut down at the plate to end the series. Who was tagged out at home to end the Giants season in 2003?
    a) Ray Durham
    b) Edgardo Alfonzo

c) Marquis Grissom
d) J.T. Snow

Q194: From all eras of franchise history, nearly 100 players had at least one game with five hits. Through 2017, only 28 of those players had multiple games with at least five hits. The franchise record is seven such games. Who had seven games with five or more hits for the Giants?
a) Ross Youngs
b) Freddie Lindstrom
c) Bill Terry
d) Frankie Frisch

Q195: Who is the only player in franchise history with two five-hit games at Candlestick Park?
a) Robby Thompson
b) Chris Speier
c) Joe Morgan
d) Gary Maddox

Q196: The 1954 World Series featured the New York Giants and Cleveland Indians. Game 1 was at the Polo Grounds. In the eighth inning, with the score tied 2-2, and with two runners on base, Willie Mays made the greatest defensive play in baseball history. His over-the-shoulder grab of a 460-foot drive to the deepest part of the park saved the game. Which Cleveland Indians hitter was robbed by Mays?
a) Vic Wertz
b) Al Rosen
c) Larry Doby
d) Bobby Avila

Q197: And a follow-up to that last question … who won Game 1 of the 1954 World Series with a pinch-hit home run in the tenth inning?
a) Davey Williams
b) Dusty Rhodes
c) Don Mueller
d) Hank Thompson

Q198: The All-Star break isn't perfectly halfway through the season, but it

is used as a first/second half split to gauge success for any number of individual and team stats. In the last 50 years, the highest hits total at the All-Star break belongs to Atlanta Braves outfielder Ralph Garr with 149. From 1958-2017, one Giant had a franchise best 120 hits at the break and earned his first All-Star selection as a result. Who had more hits at the All-Star break than any other player in San Francisco Giants history?
   a) Brett Butler
   b) Will Clark
   c) Chili Davis
   d) Rich Aurilia

Q199: And a follow-up to that last question … who unbelievably scored 70 runs before the All-Star break a franchise record four times?
   a) Bobby Bonds
   b) Barry Bonds
   c) Willie Mays
   d) Jeff Kent

Q200: In 2008, Francisco Rodriguez had a major-league record 38 saves at the All-Star break for the Los Angeles Angels of Anaheim. The most saves at the break for a Giants closer is 29. Who holds this record?
   a) Brian Wilson
   b) Rod Beck
   c) Robb Nen
   d) Matt Herges

BOTTOM OF THE TENTH—ANSWER KEY

191: b. Joe Panik.

192: a. 1936-37.

193: d. J.T. Snow.

194: c. Bill Terry.

195: a. Robby Thompson.

196: a. Vic Wertz.

197: b. Dusty Rhodes.

198: d. Rich Aurilia.

199: a. Bobby Bonds.

200: b. Rod Beck.

ABOUT THE AUTHORS

Tucker Elliot is a former teacher, coach, and athletic director. He has visited schools on four continents and more than twenty countries as a volunteer or an invited speaker/lecturer. He lives in Florida and Korea. Connect with Tucker on Amazon, Facebook, Twitter, or email: tckrelliot@gmail.com

Zac Robinson is the author of many MMA and baseball books. You can connect with Zac on Amazon, Facebook, and Twitter.

e-Books by Tucker Elliot

The Day Before 9/11

The Memory of Hope

The Rainy Season

Third Ring Children

The Other Side of the River

Baseball Books by Tucker Elliot

Baltimore Orioles IQ: The Ultimate Test of True Fandom

Cincinnati Reds IQ: The Ultimate Test of True Fandom

Major League Baseball IQ: The Ultimate Test of True Fandom

Tampa Bay Rays IQ: The Ultimate Test of True Fandom

Atlanta Braves IQ: The Ultimate Test of True Fandom

Cleveland Indians IQ: The Ultimate Test of True Fandom

New York Yankees IQ: The Ultimate Test of True Fandom

San Francisco Giants IQ: The Ultimate Test of True Fandom

Washington Nationals IQ: The Ultimate Test of True Fandom

Atlanta Braves: An Interactive Guide to the World of Sports

Boston Red Sox: An Interactive Guide to the World of Sports

San Francisco Giants: An Interactive Guide to the World of Sports

51 Questions for the Diehard Fan: New York Yankees

51 Questions for the Diehard Fan: Atlanta Braves

51 Questions for the Diehard Fan: Baltimore Orioles

e-Books by Zac Robinson

Caged Love

The Comeback

Would You ...

MMA/Baseball Books by Zac Robinson

From the Fields to the Garden: The Life of Stitch Duran

From the Fields to the Garden II

Through the Cage Door

Mixed Martial Arts IQ: The Ultimate Test of True Fandom

Ranger Up Presents Mixed Martial Arts IQ: The Ultimate Test of True Fandom, Volume II

Mixed Martial Arts: An Interactive Guide to the World of Sports

Texas Rangers: An Interactive Guide to the World of Sports

San Francisco Giants: An Interactive Guide to the World of Sports

SOURCES

Baseball-reference.com (Play Index)

MLB.com (and the official team sites through MLB.com)

BaseballHallofFame.org

ESPN.com

SABR.org

Baseball-Almanac.com

Elias Sports Bureau

BLACK MESA

Visit us on the web to learn more about Black Mesa and our authors:

www.blackmesabooks.com

Or contact us via email:

admin@blackmesabooks.com

www.ingramcontent.com/pod-product-compliance
Lightning Source LLC
Chambersburg PA
CBHW061445040426
42450CB00007B/1213